Family Spaces in Art Museums

AMERICAN ALLIANCE OF MUSEUMS

The American Alliance of Museums has been bringing museums together since 1906, helping to develop standards and best practices, gathering and sharing knowledge, and providing advocacy on issues of concern to the entire museum community. Representing more than 35,000 individual museum professionals and volunteers, institutions, and corporate partners serving the museum field, the Alliance stands for the broad scope of the museum community.

The American Alliance of Museums' mission is to champion museums and nurture excellence in partnership with its members and allies.

Books published by AAM further the Alliance's mission to make standards and best practices for the broad museum community widely available.

Family Spaces in Art Museums

Creating Curiosity, Wonder, and Play

JULIA FORBES AND MARIANNA ADAMS
WITH JEANINE ANCELET

ROWMAN & LITTLEFIELD
Lanham • Boulder • New York • London

Published by Rowman & Littlefield

An imprint of The Rowman & Littlefield Publishing Group, Inc.

4501 Forbes Boulevard, Suite 200, Lanham, Maryland 20706

www.rowman.com

86-90 Paul Street, London EC2A 4NE

British Library Cataloguing in Publication Information Available

Library of Congress Cataloging-in-Publication Data Available

ISBN 978-1-5381-4884-6 (cloth)
ISBN 978-1-5381-4885-3 (pbk.)
ISBN 978-1-5381-4886-0 (electronic)

To Maggie and Fig,
who were our furry companions as we wrote this volume.

Contents

Acknowledgments

THIS BOOK WOULD NOT HAVE BEEN POSSIBLE WITH-out the foundational research conducted from 2007 to 2011 through the Family Learning in Interactive Galleries (FLING) visitor study generously funded by the Institute for Museum and Library Services (IMLS). Their vision to support groundbreaking research that makes the work we all do better cannot be underestimated.

The FLING project was led by Anne Henderson, Director of Education and Outreach at the Frist Art Museum. She was our project manager and partner in research. She kept our work on track, and we could not have taken on the huge task of the FLING research study without her leadership. She has also been a key member of our team as we wrote this book, contributing, along with her colleague Samantha Andrews, a case study for chapter 4. At the time of the FLING project, Cynthia Moreno was at the helm of the education department at the Speed Museum of Art. The Speed completed the trio of art museums, the High Museum of Art being the third, that were the focus of the research grant. Currently the Director of Learning and Engagement at the Mint Museum in Charlotte, North Carolina, Cynthia is an inspiring and longtime colleague and critical member of our team. She wrote a case study for chapter 4 sharing the ways she used the FLING research at the Speed and how those findings have influenced her work at the Mint Museum.

The scientific research for the FLING project was led by Dr. Jessica Luke, now at the University of Washington, and Jeanine Ancelet of Audience Focus, and, of course, Dr. Marianna Adams. We are incredibly grateful for Dr. Luke's design and implementation of the large-scale Motivation, Use, Value study, together with her research assistants, Angie Ong and Claudia Figueiredo. These findings have been invaluable to the field. Ancelet was not only a key researcher on the FLING Longitudinal Case Study, with Dr. Adams, but also led the Art Lab study for the new family gallery development at the High Museum of Art in 2016. Her contributions and expertise have played a huge role in the development of this book. We are so grateful for her generosity and contributions.

As part of the FLING project, the grant allowed us to bring on three full-time evaluation assistants, one at each museum site. These colleagues, Gwendolyn Kelly at the Speed Museum of Art, Sofia Fredin Broman at the High Museum of Art, and Kim Jameson at the Frist Art Museum, conducted research and, in particular, spent eighteen months with the seventeen families that agreed to be shadowed as part of the Longitudinal Case Study. We are grateful to all of them for the part they each played in this critical research, foundational to the content of this book.

Kelly left the Speed Art Museum in 2013 and continued to facilitate community workshops with several arts organizations, as well as in the education department of KET, the local PBS affiliate. She is currently contracted by the Fund for the Arts to manage two community public arts–focused projects. She says, "The FLING experience of watching families in public learning environments and talking with them about it verified the importance of family-based programming and strengthened my belief that families should consciously learn together in enriched environments."

Sofia Broman moved back to Sweden shortly after 2011 and has since started a family of her own. She is the Business Manager Art for the Stockholm Public Transport's (SL) public art collection, known as "the world's longest art gallery." The Stockholm subway features 250 artists in ninety-four of the city's one hundred stations, transforming public spaces into an aesthetic experience. Broman notes, "My work on the FLING project influenced the way I design family art tours in the SL transit system, emphasizing the importance of providing experiences for parents, children, and grandparents."

Kim Jameson moved to Australia in 2013 and since then has worked for local government and not-for-profit organizations. All her roles have involved capacity building within and among cultural communities, arts organizations, and individuals. Jameson says, "I have applied all aspects of the FLING learning across all my roles, creating projects, programs, and environments that are accessible to a wide range of people, cultures, and experiences."

We are deeply grateful to each of the members of the seventeen families who agreed to be part of the FLING study. Their commitment of time and their candor in talking about how they felt about their museum experiences and what that meant to their families made our findings and learnings richer than we could have imagined. A special thanks to the three families for answering our call when we reached back out to them in 2021 to hear how they were influenced by museums, the arts, and participation in our study.

We would like to thank Patricia Rodewald who, during the research study, was the Eleanor McDonald Storza Director of Education at the High Museum of Art. She was a key member of the FLING team. Her support then and now as we embarked on the book project has been so important. She has been a sounding board and thinking partner. Currently Rodewald is living and working in China as a museum consultant. The findings from the FLING study have been introduced to museum educators in China, influencing the development of many family experiences in a variety of museums.

Our sincerest thanks go to Virginia Shearer, the former Eleanor McDonald Storza Director of Educa-

tion at the High Museum of Art, for encouraging us to take this on this book project. She championed our work and encouraged us to submit the proposal to the American Alliance of Museums in 2019. She has been a terrific cheerleader for this work and a truly wonderful colleague.

Dean Phelus, the senior director for leadership programs and special events at the American Alliance of Museums, allowed us the opportunity to publish this book and supported us through the early proposal stages of this project. We are grateful for his leadership and vision. At Rowman & Littlefield, we thank Charles Harmon, senior executive editor, and Erinn Slanina, editorial assistant, for shepherding new authors through what seemed to us like a daunting undertaking. Charles, your wise counsel and guidance through this process made a huge difference for us.

Our thanks go to Rand Suffolk, the Nancy and Holcombe T. Green, Jr., Director of the High Museum of Art, for his support of this book project and for taking the time to write the foreword.

Finally, we thank Julia's parents, Fred and Betty Forbes, for carefully reading the manuscript and providing a fresh set of "general public" eyes. They have always been Julia's biggest supporters and she is deeply grateful for them.

Foreword

In October 1968, the High Museum of Art introduced its first dedicated space for families to learn, play, and explore. The first installation was called *Color/Light/Color* (1968–1971) and explored the nature, properties, and uses of color. Gudmund Vigtel, director of the museum from 1963 to 1991, and a key figure in the High's history, once reflected: "My proudest accomplishment to date is the Junior Activities Center established within the museum. . . . children are the art audiences of the future. The more knowledgeable they are, the greater the dialog[ue] possible between the community and the museum."

Nearly fifty years later, Vigtel's conviction that children were central to the mission, relevance, and sustainability of the museum continued to resonate. In fact, from its initial iteration as the Junior Activities Center to its current identity as the Greene Family Learning Gallery, this family-focused, interactive space evolved and remains a signature aspect of a child's visit. This book demonstrates how transformative an interactive family space can be to an art museum.

For the High Museum in 2016, the time was right—strategically and operationally—to re-vision our space again in conjunction with a concurrent reinstallation of our permanent collection galleries in 2018. Our goal was to deliver an entirely new platform of family engagement. Our challenge was to do so in a fashion that embraced and expressed our core institutional values: Growth, Inclusivity, Collaboration, and Connectivity. To accomplish that, the new Greene Family Learning Gallery was conceptually informed by thought leaders from the fields of early learning and design thinking, as well as the incorporation of sensitivities, insights, and needs of various advocacy groups within our community. The result proved to be a compelling, intergenerational, and remarkably accessible articulation of our aspirations.

Consequently, we are grateful for the opportunity to share our journey as part of this volume. We also hope this publication, as well as the practical outcomes of our experience, will prove useful for creating your own space and will affirm your commitment to families as primary drivers of institutional impact and sustainability.

Rand Suffolk
Nancy and Holcombe T. Green, Jr.,
Director, High Museum of Art

ABOUT RAND SUFFOLK

Rand Suffolk is the Nancy and Holcombe T. Green, Jr., Director of the High Museum of Art. Since his arrival in 2015, he has championed a renewed commitment to community engagement, placing emphasis on collaboration, inclusivity, and access. Prior to joining the High, Suffolk served as director of Philbrook Museum of Art in Tulsa, Oklahoma, where he designed and implemented a comprehensive plan that aligned the institution's programming with the interests of Tulsa residents. His successful institutional strategy and program was nationally recognized in a 2013 study led by independent researchers Anne Bergeron and Beth Tuttle in partnership with the American Alliance of Museums (AAM), in which Philbrook was highlighted as one of six national models of community engagement. From 1999 through 2007, Suffolk was the director of the Hyde Collection Art Museum in Glens Falls, New York. Suffolk has curated more than twenty-five exhibitions and has participated as a juror, panel member, or guest lecturer for a variety of art-related organizations and programs. He holds a master's degree in art history from Bryn Mawr College, a master's degree in higher education administration from Columbia University, and a Bachelor of Arts degree from Connecticut College.

Preface

In 2005 educators from the High Museum of Art in Atlanta, Georgia (Julia Forbes), and the Frist Art Museum in Nashville, Tennessee (Anne Henderson), along with, Marianna Adams, a museum evaluator with deep experience in family research, made a presentation[1] at the Getty Museum conference "From Content to Play: Family-Oriented Interactive Spaces in Art and History Museums."[2] As we listened to the presentations and talked with colleagues during breaks, we realized that there was a gap in the research on how families use and value such spaces, so an idea was hatched for a multiyear study across three art museums in the southeastern United States that had a strong track record of creating interactive spaces for families. We invited Cynthia Moreno, who was head of education at the Speed Museum of Art in Louisville, Kentucky, at the time, to join the team. This group applied for and received a National Leadership Grant in 2007 from the Institute for Museum and Library Services (IMLS) for a four-year extensive research initiative across these three museums, and we partnered with two visitor research companies—Marianna Adams and Jeanine Ancelet of Audience Focus and Jessica Luke of the Institute for Learning Innovation (ILI). The IMLS-funded research study was completed in 2011 and to date is only published online at www.artmuseumfamilyspaces.org.

We named the collaborative research project *Family Learning in Interactive Galleries* (FLING), and its overarching goal was to better understand how and in what ways interactive art museum experiences enhance family learning.

The research consisted of an extensive literature review, which guided our research design. Two separate but interrelated studies were developed: the Motivational, Use, Value Large-Scale study (MUV) led by Dr. Luke and the Longitudinal Case Study (LCS) led by Adams and Ancelet. This design investigated both a broad and deep, tightly focused view of families in art museum interactive spaces.

For the MUV study, the research questions were:

1. Who are the families/intergenerational groups (IGGs) that visit interactive art museum spaces?
2. What do families/IGGs do on their visit?
3. How do families/IGGs benefit from the interactive experience?

At the end of their museum visit, families were invited to complete a family puzzle reflection, an opportunity for them to reconstruct their visit to the museum using iconic photographs of the interactive space, ancillary interactive resources (e.g., backpacks), museum collections, exhibitions, and amenities (i.e., café, shop). This was not only a fun experience for the families, but it also allowed us to accurately pinpoint where during the visit families visited the interactive galleries. Our research assistants followed up with a brief interview and a written survey that sought information about benefits of the experience to children, parents, and the family group. A post-post online survey was sent to a subsample of families.

The LCS sought rich and nuanced information about families in art museums through the following research questions:

1. Who are the families who use interactive spaces in art museums?
2. How do families use interactive spaces in art museums?
3. What is the value of interactive spaces in art museums for families?
4. How does the value of interactive spaces in art museums intersect with and support frequent-visiting families' core values?

This study used ethnographic tools and strategies to better understand how families learn in interactive art spaces, how those experiences enhance their overall museum visit, and how the museum experience contributes, in general, to family learning. Six families at each of the three museum partner sites (for a total of eighteen families) were recruited to participate. The research assistant at each museum accompanied families on three visits to the art museum and three visits to other family learning destinations of the family's choice. We brought the families together three times for member checks at each museum during the eighteen months of data collection. Data from the observations, interviews, and field notes were subjected to layers of content analysis, looking for patterns within and across families.

Our final phase of the project was to develop an online toolkit as a resource for practitioners archived at www.artmuseumfamilyspaces.org.

Since that groundbreaking research, all the team members, educators, and researchers have made extensive use of the findings in their practice. The High and the Frist opened newly reinstalled family spaces in 2018 that directly applied our research findings. The Mint Museum primarily applies lessons learned through the research to their short-term (three to six months) interactive experiences that are integrated within changing exhibitions or parts of the permanent collection. We have all continued to conduct additional visitor research working closely with our well-established team. When the American Alliance of Museums reached out to the field requesting book proposals in 2019, we thought it was finally time to put all we have learned into writing, bring our 2011 study up to date, and share it more formally and more widely with our colleagues.

The family visitor is an important and, in fact, critical audience for art museums. Museums use many different strategies to reach families—family days and festivals, workshops, special tours, family backpacks, gallery guides, family-focused labels, in-gallery materials, demonstration carts—but none of those approaches are a larger financial or space-grabbing commitment than an interactive family gallery. So why should you do it? Simply, because families matter to the health of your institution.

In 2006, *Parents* magazine did a survey to assess the family-friendliness of US art museums. They identified thirty art museums as the best for families. Almost half of those had special interactive galleries for families. In 2011 our IMLS-funded study sought a deeper understanding of why families visit and what they value about interactive spaces in art museums. Throughout this book, we will reveal what we found. And in 2019, a study conducted by Colleen Dilenschneider of the blog, *Know Your Own Bone*,[3] dem-

onstrated how critical it is to bring children to the art museum in a family group and how that fosters lifelong museum visitors. To share a powerful example, a past president of the board of directors at the High Museum of Art shared that his first memory of the High Museum was in the High's family interactive installation, *The City* (1974–1978) and what a powerful impact playing there had on him.

WHO IS THIS BOOK FOR?

Family Spaces in Art Museums: Creating Curiosity, Wonder, and Play shares insights, best practices, and lessons learned from years of experience in creating dedicated spaces for families in a wide range of art museums. We know this book will be a valuable resource for museum educators in art museums, but we hope colleagues in marketing and development, as well as directors and board members, will find the material equally meaningful. Educators working in other museum disciplines like children's museums, science centers, and history museums may also find tips and strategies that will make their work more impactful. The book identifies key issues that all museum professionals need to consider when developing interactive family spaces. Each chapter is situated within visitor research findings and how practicing museum educators have used those findings to better understand the family audience and develop fun, safe, and inclusive spaces that inspire wonder and curiosity, as well as places for meaning-making and family bonding, all in the service of creating loyal and committed lifelong museum visitors.

WHAT TO EXPECT FROM THIS BOOK

We have organized the book to be a how-to guide to creating or updating your interactive family space—everything you need to know, soup to nuts, from understanding your audience to hiring a designer and opening your doors to the public. In the first chapter, "Know Your Audience," we define what a family is to us. We delve into the family as a museum audience. Who are they? Why do they come to a museum? What are they looking for? In chapter 2, "Values Matter," we unpack our four years of IMLS-funded research revealing what families value about a museum experience. What is their motivation for coming? We also tackle the question of what museums should value about families. Early in our research for the IMLS grant we conducted a survey of the field around family spaces. In 2020 we reached back to many of these participants asking museum educators how valuable the family audience is to their institution and why. We explore why the family is such an important audience that warrants dedicated spaces and specially crafted experiences. Chapter 3, "Stop, Look, Listen," takes a deep dive into how families use interactive spaces and how understanding that impacts how you develop the activities and design the spaces. Chapter 4, "Walk the Talk," presents three case studies from museum educators with deep experience in creating and running more than one interactive space over many years of practice. Here's where we illustrate how we have put our theory into practice. We hope this personal experience, counsel, and advice from practicing professionals provides inspiration, best practices, and tips and tricks that will save you time, money, and a few missteps. Finally, chapter 5, "Get Started," is our step-by-step guide to reinstall or create a new interactive family space in an art museum. It is filled with specific ideas and tools that will guide you through the complicated process of creating a meaningful space that inspires curiosity, wonder, and play.

As you embark on the huge task of creating an interactive space for families at your museum be sure you and your team approach the work with intentionality. In this book we encourage you to listen to your visitors and understand what they want. Talk to your community; invite them into the process. But equally important is *your* attitude about the work. Bring a sense of curiosity and wonder to your project. Tap into the playful side of yourself as you and your team consider the goals and vision for your space. These qualities of curiosity, wonder, and play will permeate your space if you let them guide you as you create.

NOTES

1. https://www.getty.edu/education/symposium/Forbes .pdf.
2. https://www.getty.edu/education/museum_educators/ content_play.html.
3. https://www.colleendilen.com/2019/09/04/school -group-vs-family-visitors-which-kids-come-back-as -adults-data/.

CHAPTER 1

Know Your Audience

MUSEUMS ARE POWERFUL PLACES FOR FAMILY LEARN-
ing. They offer unique contexts in which families
spend quality time talking and drawing on individual
and collective memories to make sense of the world
around them.[1] However, as the number of families
visiting museums continued to increase over the past
two decades, research on the nature and value of the
family learning experience in museums, particularly
art museums, did not keep pace.[2] To address that
gap, in 2007 a group of art museum educators and
evaluation professions gathered together determined
to learn more because we all strongly believed it was
critical for museums to better understand the nature
of family audiences and the museum's role in facilitating quality intergenerational learning.

At the time, much of what was known about family
learning in museums came from studies conducted in
science centers and children's museums.[3] There was
little research focused on families in art museums,
despite that more than 90 percent of art museums
nationwide offer specialized programming for families.[4] Increasing numbers of art museums were targeting families through interactive experiences. Many
such programs were family-based events in galleries
or a studio space designed to encourage parents and
children to engage with works of art together. But we
started to notice a powerful trend: Many art museums
were developing dedicated spaces for families. So,
as educators at the Speed Art Museum (Art Sparks
Interactive Gallery), Frist Center for the Visual Arts,
now the Frist Art Museum (Martin ArtQuest gallery),
and the High Museum of Art (Greene Family Learning Gallery), we decided it was time to get serious and
get some real data. We asked Audience Focus and the
Institute for Learning Innovation to join us and we received a four-year Institute for Museums and Library
Services (IMLS)-funded research grant. We called our
project Family Learning in Interactive Galleries or
FLING. In 2011 we published our research through
a website.[5] Now we are thrilled to gather what we
learned in the FLING study and from other research

conducted since then, together with what we have
learned in our practice since the study ended, into
a user-friendly book for museum professionals who
either want to establish their first dedicated interactive space, reinstall an existing space, or experiment
with temporary interactive areas within exhibitions
or collections.

The interactive spaces featured in this book are
the Frist Art Museum Martin ArtQuest's 2001–2018
installation and 2018 to present installation; the High
Museum of Art Greene Family Learning Gallery's
2005–2018 installation and 2018 to present installation; and the Speed Art Museum Art Sparks 1997–
2005 installation and 2005–2012 installation.

WHAT IS A FAMILY?

To best serve a family audience, museum practitioners need to be clear about their own perceptions
and sometimes misconceptions around what a family is and is not. What constitutes a family today
has become increasingly complex, with definitions of
"family" varying widely. Society has expanded on the
traditional mid-twentieth-century notion of the nu-
clear family consisting of a mother, father, and a few
children, to include blended families, single-parent
families, and families of choice. Regardless of whether
we grow up in a "happy" or not-so-happy family, a
family is probably the most fundamental social organization in which every human is involved.

The variety in the structure of families in the twenty-
first century can present problems for museum practitioners and researchers. Falk and Dierking[6] have
turned the responsibility of describing family over to
the research participants, saying that a family is made
up of persons who define themselves as such. Because
of this shift in thinking, museum practitioners and
researchers tend to refer to family groups as intergenerational, cross-generational, or multigenerational
groups, thereby avoiding the traditional notion that
a family consists only of immediate family members
related by blood or marriage.

Family isn't always blood. It's the people in your life who want you in theirs; the ones who accept you for who you are. The ones that would do anything to see you smile and who love you no matter what.[7]

Another issue that emerges when trying to define a family has to do with the age range. When museum educators and researchers think about an intergenerational group they often envision at least one adult and one or more children age fifteen or younger. Yet, isn't an all-adult group of older adults with their grown children also an intergenerational family? This is why it is important for museum educators, as well as researchers, to be clear about the audience they are calling a family. It's not a question of right or wrong but a question of clarity. Practitioners must decide who their target audience is and define that clearly as they plan for any type of family programming.

If family groups are no longer easily defined by blood relation or living situation, how can museum educators and researchers distinguish them from nonfamily social groups? One key element is that fam-

ilies closely resemble, and are sometimes described as, "communities of learning" or "communities of practice." By defining families within these categories, we emphasize the importance of social interaction through which families learn, as well as a family's tendency to work toward the same goals. Family groups have been described as microcommunities, sharing values, beliefs, history, customs, language, vocabulary, understandings, and assumptions (figure 1.1). As communities of learners, families work together to support learning and the transfer of information among its members.

For children, the family is the first and often most influential learning group within their life. Through conversations and social interactions, family members young and old continuously learn from each other. They talk about what they see, hear, and read, relating it to their previous experiences and memories, and model behavior and actions for one another. This is not to say that all members within one family are homogeneous in their knowledge, personal experiences, or preferred learning styles. In fact, individual

Figure 1.1.   Families come in all shapes, sizes, and configurations. Used by permission: Marianna Adams, Photographer

family members will likely bring a range of education, learning skills, and life experiences to a museum visit. However, when a family group visits the museum together, they will function as a multigenerational, social learning group and typically attach great importance to that social interaction.

When creating experiences for families in museums and when evaluating the effectiveness of those experiences, practitioners and researchers must carefully define what constitutes a family. Typically, our programming and research is based on a concept of the family that doesn't accurately match the families we see at the museum.

> Viewing families as overlapping networks that extend across multiple households, with each network having at its nucleus a reference person, might yield new insights, especially in an era when families are becoming more complex and difficult to classify. Because only a small number of family scholars have adopted this approach, the potential of taking people's families-of-choice seriously is currently unrealized.[8]

FAMILIES IN MUSEUMS

Despite the prevalence of interactive family galleries in art museums, when we began the FLING study in 2007,[9] little was known about who used them or how they benefit from the experience. A handful of unpublished evaluation studies in this area hinted at the rich potential of family galleries in art museums to contribute to intergenerational learning; however, they were not generalizable given their situational focus on one museum and its family experience. In fact, at the time, there was little research focused on families in art museums at all, despite the reality that most art museums nationwide offer specialized programming for families and more and more art museums provide interactive experiences or family-friendly interpretation such as audio guides and tours.

Since 2011, when we completed the FLING study, there has not been much additional research on families in art museums.[10] There are articles and book chapters that herald the value of the museum for young children and blogs and how-to articles that describe ways museums can be more family friendly, many of them quite interesting and helpful. Although a few of these articles might cite one research source, they usually cite no research to back up their opinions.

Social Interaction Is Key

Because families operate as a social unit, it is not surprising that they spend a majority of their time at the museum engaged in social interaction and conversation, sharing what they know and trying to learn more about each other and the world around them.[11]

> Families are the main context of learning for most people. Learning within the family is usually more lasting and influential than any other. Family life provides a foundation and context for all learning.[12]

Each family member benefits from interacting socially with the larger family group. So does such interaction result in learning or is simply a mechanism through which learning happens and conversations lead to increased learning?[13] We have observed, and studies support us, that social interaction between family members not only leads to increased cognitive understanding of exhibition-related concepts and themes but also leads to the development of shared knowledge, memories, and family history, as well as to an increased understanding of each other.[14]

Certain types of verbal and nonverbal social interactions are associated with learning in general.[15] The most common learning behaviors include asking and answering questions, providing descriptions, offering explanations, directing and orienting, pointing, observing, and modeling, pretending or role-playing, providing clues or making suggestions, creating and presenting work, and offering reinforcement.

Asking and answering questions is a type of social behavior observed among family groups in museums.[16] Both parents and children engage in the inquiry process, often asking questions about the exhibitions, programs, and each other. Adults often pose guiding questions about where to go, what to see, and how to do something. One study found that parents visiting a science museum with "expert children" often present questions that encourage "knowledge rehearsal" and offer positive reinforcement for their children's "knowledge performance."[17] Family members try to enhance the family learning experience by providing descriptions, interpreting information, and offering explanations or hypotheses.[18] Another study found that different tiers or "learning levels" are embedded within these types of family conversations, which include "identifying," "describing," and "interpreting and applying."[19]

Families engage in conversations that link their recent museum experience with their previous knowledge and experiences, and the family as a whole, or individuals in the group, often find ways to talk about what they are seeing or doing in the museum in relation to prior experience such as school, other museum visits, television or movies, and other family experiences.[20] Adults and children who have visited museums frequently in the past often recount previous museum experiences with their family members. For example, in a study of grandparent-child family groups, it was found that children are "eager to show their grandparents what they know from previous visit[s] to the museum."[21] Parents and grandparents have also been observed engaged in similar behaviors, such as passing down stories of former experiences, nostalgia, and memories to children.[22]

Keep in mind that these family groups are not necessarily deliberate about or even totally conscious of these social interaction behaviors. Adults who engage in this kind of back-and-forth inquiry usually learned from seeing the behavior modeled, either in their own families or with friends or schoolteachers. Nevertheless, there are strong studies that support the importance of back-and-forth conversation, or talking *with* children rather than *at* them, in a young child's brain development.[23]

Decision Makers

As is the case with who decides to visit the museum in the first place, who drives the visit once in the museum varies. Some studies point toward the child, others point to the adult, and some studies find both adults and children sharing in the decision-making equally. Some parents allow children to follow their own interests and curiosity and to use the museum to explore and make discoveries.[24] Children, especially young children, also tend to be the driving force behind activities that are not directly associated with exhibit viewing, such as visiting the museum store, eating, or using the bathroom.[25] Sometimes adults and children share the responsibility for negotiating the course of the visit, and in most instances, families try to do and see things that all members of the family will find enjoyable and interesting.[26]

Fewer studies have looked at decision-making in terms of ending a visit to the museum. An ethnographic study of families in science museums found that leave-taking is most often instigated by one of the children in the family, and in particular, it is often the youngest child who asks to leave. In addition, parents also instigate leave-taking, but the social interplay that occurs when a parent initiates the departure versus when a child initiates, looks quite different. When one of the children asks to leave, there is generally some appeal such as, "can we go now," or "I'm hungry," or "I'm tired." Whereas, when a parent makes a decision to leave "there is no appeal of 'can we go now,' but instead a statement establishing the end of the activity."[27]

Who Does What?

Understanding the different roles and responsibilities family members assume while engaged in learning conversations and behaviors during a museum visit can be a powerful tool for the museum practitioner.[28] Teaching is usually a reciprocal activity that all family members engage in, even though each family member might contribute for different reasons and during different contexts.[29] Although significant differences exist in the ways parents versus children behave, the similarities tend to outweigh the differences.[30] In a study of families at the Children's Museum of Indianapolis, all family members engaged somewhat equally with each other. Adults asked children questions; children asked adults questions; and children interacted with one another as did adults with other adults.[31]

Of course, not all parents and children engage in teaching or learning behaviors equally. Some parents are more actively involved in supporting or teaching roles, and sometimes children will take on more active teaching roles than parents if the child is considered more knowledgeable on a subject.[32] Interestingly the person who ends up providing the most information during a museum visit cannot be predetermined by the person's status in the family (parent or child, mother or father), but, rather, the family group "actively negotiates who will provide information depending on who is the most knowledgeable about a presented topic."[33]

Parents differ in the level of guidance they extend to their children. Some parents have clear strategies for helping their children solve problems and understand exhibition components, while other parents tend to let their children explore on their own and provide assistance only when the child asks for it.[34] As museum professionals, we find the following eight types of adult caregivers or parental behaviors extremely helpful when thinking about designing effective family experiences in the museum.[35]

1. Caretaker: adults who keep surveillance but allow children to explore freely;
2. Supporter: adults who provide support without interference;
3. Helper: adults who help out only as much as required so that children can take over as much as possible;
4. Initiator: adults who initiate the activity and then pass it over to the children;

5. Assistant – adults who act as an extra pair of hands for children who take the lead;
6. Partner: adults who act as equal partners with children throughout an activity;
7. Leader: adults who lead activities throughout, only allowing minor contributions from the children; and
8. Demonstrator: adults who carry out the entire activity by themselves while children watch.

FAMILY LEARNING IN INTERACTIVE SPACES IN ART MUSEUMS

The FLING study took two parallel approaches to the research, one large-scale and quantitative (Motivation, Use, and Value Study [MUV])[36] and the other small-scale and qualitative (Longitudinal Case Study [LCS]).[37]

The LCS was made up of seventeen committed families across the three museums that were willing to spend a year with us. Each museum recruited six families to observe for eighteen months. The families were representative of the diversity of art museum family visitors at that museum. The children in the project ranged in age from three to thirteen years (one child of at least five to twelve years of age was required to participate in the study), and the families included a grandmother, a mother in the military, a mother who owned a business, and a father who was an artist. The children were in public and private schools, as well as homeschooled. The families were asked to visit their local art museum three times and make three visits to other comparable institutions or locations during the year of the study. The on-site researcher for each institution became like an "auntie," accompanying the families during the visits. They also conducted in-depth, semi-structured follow-up interviews with the families a week or so after each of the six visits.

Families participating in the MUV study, on the other hand, targeted adults who were part of an intergenerational group, defined as any group of two or more people with at least one adult and one child younger than age twelve; had visited the interactive space in the museum with their group; and were not part of an organized visit or tour (i.e., they should have had the opportunity to explore the museum on their own and not on a guided tour such as might happen with scout or church groups).

Our Assumptions Going in

We thought these two groups of visitors (the LCS focus on families who frequently visit museums and the MUV study focus on the general population of family visitors in the three museums) might have different needs and values. But that was not the case; they looked the same on all measures. It was one of the most surprising and exciting results of our work, making clear that our findings were solidly supported. When we looked at who the families were that were visiting our three interactive galleries we were able to generalize to the larger population of art museum visitors. That's the big value of this research and what was missing in many other studies!

Characteristics of Family Visitors to Interactive Spaces

When we overlapped the results of the two studies, we were able to conclude that the majority of family visitors had the following characteristics. They were family groups comprised of three to four people on average, usually moms, often with multiple children in tow. They wanted to expose their children to art and creative endeavors and to enjoy doing that together as a family group. The adults were primarily frequent museum goers and considered themselves art enthusiasts. More than 70 percent identified themselves as people who create art for enjoyment and more than 50 percent had taken art classes in the past. They tended to be regular visitors to museums of all types, with 25 to 40 percent of them having a membership at the museum. More than 46 percent of the respondents were first-time visitors and more than 46 percent were repeat visitors from two to nine times in the past year. Most of the study participants were familiar with the interactive space, meaning they had either heard about it or been before.[38]

TYPICAL CHARACTERISTICS OF INTERGENERATIONAL GROUPS[39]

- Groups comprised of three to four people
- Usually women with multiple children
- Mostly immediate family members
- Frequent museum visitors
- Interested in art
- Familiar with existence of the interactive space, both first-time and repeat visitors

---

A better understanding of who our visitors are has had an immeasurable impact on our practice as museum educators. It helps us to specifically direct our marketing efforts in areas that will help us to build our family audience. It has not only informed the redesign of our interactive spaces but is also considered in all the family programs we create. Learn more about how we used the study results in chapter 4.

YOUR TURN

As you consider revising or creating your own family interactive space or family programming, consider having spirited discussions with your museum colleagues around the following questions:

- What is your working definition of a family? Does that change depending on the type of experience or program you develop? If yes, how so?
- What do you know about the families who currently visit your museum? What percentage of your visitors are families? Is this information based on your experience and observation or from studies you have conducted? What do you want to know about families who visit your museum?
- What do you know about why families do *not* put your museum on their list of family outing options? If you don't know much, how could you find out more?

NOTES

1. Ash, 2003; Crowley, et al., 2001.
2. Ellenbogen, Luke, and Dierking, 2004.
3. Ash, 2003; Borun and Dritsas, 1996; Borun, Dritsas, Johnson, et al., 1998; Crowley, et al., 2001; Ellenbogen, et al., 2004.
4. Wetterlund and Sayre, 2003.
5. www.famliesinartmuseums.org.
6. Falk and Dierking, 2000.
7. Unknown author.
8. Amato, 2014.
9. *Family Learning in Interactive Galleries*, 2010.
10. For example, Munley, 2012, and Denver Art Museum, 2013.
11. Dierking, 1989; Dierking, Luke, and Falk, 2002; Laetsch, Diamond, Gottfried, and Rosenfeld, 1980; Wolf and Wood, 2012.
12. *Riches Beyond Price: Making the Most of Family Learning*, NIACE, 1995.
13. Adams, Luke, and Moussouri, 2004; Borun, et al., 1998; Diamond, 1986; Kelly, Savage, Griffin, and Tonkin, 2004; Laetsch, et al., 1980.
14. Blud, 1990; Borun, et al., 1998; Dierking, et al., 2002; Ellenbogen, Luke, and Dierking, 2004; Kelly, et al., 2004.
15. Beaumont and Sterry, 2005; Borun, Cleghorn, and Garfield, 1995; Borun, et al., 1998; Diamond, 1986; Dierking, 1989; Gaskins, 2008; Hilke, 1989; Moussouri, 2003; Ash, 2003.
16. Amsel and Goodwin, 2004; Borun, et al., 1995, 1998; Dierking, et al., 2002; Hooper-Greenhill, Dodd, Moussouri, et al., 2003; Kropf, 1989; McManus, 1994; Moussouri, 2003; Palmquist and Crowley, 2007; Ash, 2003.

17. Palmquist and Crowley, 2007, 801.
18. Borun, et al., 1995, 1998; Dierking, et al., 2002; Hilke, 1989; Hooper-Greenhill, et al., 2003; Kropf, 1989; Luke and Adams, 2007; McManus, 1994; Moussouri, 2003; Ash, 2003.
19. Borun, et al., 1998, 15.
20. Dierking, 1989; Dierking, et al., 2002; Kelly, et al., 2004; Kropf, 1989; Amsel and Goodwin, 2004; Crowley and Jacobs, 2002.
21. Beaumont and Sterry, 2005, 172.
22. Beaumont and Sterry, 2005.
23. Barshay, 2018.
24. Borun, et al., 1998; Kelly, et al., 2004; Stein and Luke, 2006.
25. Kropf, 1989; Moussouri, 1996.
26. Hilke, 1989; Moussouri, 1996.
27. Ellenbogen, 2004.
28. Beaumont and Sterry, 2005; Brown, 1995; Diamond, 1986; Dierking, et al., 2002; Gaskins, 2008; Gerety, 2007; Kelly, et al., 2004; Kropf, 1989; McManus, 1994; Palmquist and Crowley, 2007; Moussouri, 2003; Sterry, 2004; Ash, 2003.
29. Kropf, 1989.
30. Hilke, 1989.
31. Dierking, et al., 2002, 7.
32. Diamond, 1986; McManus, 1994; Palmquist and Crowley, 2007; Ash, 2003.
33. Palmquist and Crowley, 2007, 786.
34. Kelly, et al., 2004.
35. Brown, 1995.
36. Luke, Ong, and Figueiredo, 2011a, 2011b, 2011c.
37. Adams and Ancelet, 2011.
38. Luke, et al., 2011a.
39. Luke, et al., 2011a.

REFERENCES

Adams, M., and J. Ancelet. *Family Learning in Interactive Galleries Research Project: Three-Museum Case Study Summary*. Technical research report. Annapolis, MD: Institute for Learning Innovation, 2011. www.artmuseumfamilyspaces.org.

Adams, M., J. Luke, and J. Ancelet. *What We Do and Do Not Know about Family Learning in Art Museum Interactive Spaces: A Literature Review*. 2008. Accessed July 23, 2020, at www.artmuseumfamilyspaces.org.

Adams, M., J. Luke, and T. Moussouri. "Interactivity: Moving beyond Terminology." *Curator*, no. 47(2) (2004): 155–70.

Alexander, T., and P. Clyne. "Riches Beyond Price: Making the Most of Family Learning. A NIACE Policy Discussion Paper." (1995).

Amato, P. R. "What Is a Family?" *National Council on Family Relations*. 2014. Accessed July 21, 2020, at https://www.ncfr.org/ncfr-report/past-issues/summer-2014/what-family.

Amsel, E., and L. Goodwin. "Making Meaning Together: Family Literacy and Museums." *Journal of Museum Education*, no. 29(1) (2004): 19–23.

Ash, D. "Dialogic Inquiry in Life Science Conversations of Family Groups in a Museum." *Journal of Research in Science Teaching*, no. 40(2) (2003): 138–62.

Barshay, J. "Why Talking—and Listening—to Your Child Could Be Key to Brain Development." *The Hechinger Report*. March 12, 2018. Accessed September 29, 2020, at https://hechingerreport.org/why-talking-and-listening-to-your-child-could-be-key-to-brain-development/.

Beaumont, E., and P. Sterry. "A Study of Grandparents and Grandchildren as Visitors to Museums and Art Galleries in the UK." *Museums and Society*, no. 3(3) (2005): 167–80.

Blud, L. M. "Social Interaction and Learning among Family Groups Visiting a Museum." *Museum Management and Curatorship*, no. 9 (1990): 43–52.

Borun, M., A. Cleghorn, and C. Garfield. "Family Learning in Museums: A Bibliographic Review." *Curator*, no. 38(4) (1995): 262–70.

Borun, M., J. Dritsas, J. I. Johnson, et al. *Family Learning in Museums: The PISEC Perspective*. Philadelphia, PA: The Franklin Institute, 1998.

Brown, C. "Making the Most of Family Visits: Some Observations of Parents with Children in a Museum Science Centre." *Museum Management and Curatorship*, no. 14(1) (1995): 65–71.

Crowley, K., M. A. Callanan, J. L. Jipson, J. Galco, K. Topping, and J. Shrager. "Shared Scientific Thinking in Everyday Parent-child Activity." *Science Education*, no. 85(6) (2001): 712–32.

Crowley, K., and M. Jacobs. "Building Islands of Expertise in Everyday Family Activity." In Leinhardt, Crowley, and Knutson, eds., *Learning Conversations in Museums*, 333–56. Mahwah, NJ: Lawrence Erlbaum Associates, Inc., 2002.

Denver Art Museum. *Kids & Their Grownups: New Insights on Developing Dynamic Museum Experiences for the Whole Family*. 2013. Accessed July 22, 2020, at https://denverartmuseum.org/about/research-reports.

Diamond, J. "The Behavior of Family Groups in Science Museums." *Curator*, no. 29(2) (1986): 139–54.

Dierking, L. "The Family Museum Experience: Implications from Research." *Journal of Museum Education*, no. 14(2) (1989): 9–11.

Dierking, L., and J. Falk. "Family Behavior and Learning in Informal Science Settings: A Review of the Research." *Science Education*, no. 78(1) (1994): 57–72.

Dierking, L., J. Luke, and J. Falk. *The Children's Museum of Indianapolis: Family Learning Initiative* (unpublished evaluation report). Annapolis, MD: Institute for Learning Innovation, 2002.

Ellenbogen, K. *From Dioramas to the Dinner Table: An Ethnographic Case Study of the Role of Science Museums in Family Life*. Dissertations Abstracts International, 64(03) 846A. University Microfilms No. AAT30-85758, 2002.

Ellenbogen, K., J. Luke, and L. Dierking. "Family Learning Research in Museums: An Emerging Disciplinary Matrix." *Science Education*, no. 88(S1) (January 2004): S48–S58.

Falk, J., and L. Dierking. *Learning from Museums: Visitor Experiences and the Making of Meaning*. Walnut Creek, CA: AltaMira Press, 2000.

Family Learning in Interactive Galleries, 2010. Accessed July 23, 2020, at www.artmuseumfamilyspaces.org.

Gaskins, S. "Designing Exhibitions to Support Families' Cultural Understandings." *Exhibitionist*, no. 27(1) (2008): 11–19.

Gerety Folk, K. "Family Learning in Art Museums." In P. Vileneuve, ed., *From Periphery to Center: Art Museum Education in the 21st Century*, 110–15. Reston, VA: National Art Education Association, 2007.

Hilke, D. D. "The Family as a Learning System: An Observational Study of Families in Museums." In B. Butler and M. Sussman, eds., *Museum Visits and Activities for Family Life Enrichment*, 101–27. London: Hayworth Press, 1989.

Hooper-Greenhill, E., J. Dodd, T. Moussouri, et al. *Measuring the Outcomes and Impact of Learning in Museums, Archives and Libraries: The Learning Impact Research Project* (end of project paper). Leicester: Research Centre for Museums and Galleries, 2003.

Kelly, L., G. Savage, J. Griffin, and S. Tonkin. *Knowledge Quest: Australian Families Visit Museums*. Sydney: Australian Museum & the National Museum of Australia, 2004.

Kropf, M. B. "The Family Museum Experience: A Review of the Literature." *Journal of Museum Education*, no. 14(2) (1989): 5–8.

Laetsch, W., J. Diamond, J. Gottfried, and S. Rosenfeld. "Children and Family Groups in Science Centers." *Science and Children*, no. 17(6) (1980): 14–17.

Luke, J., and M. Adams. "What Research Says about Learning in Art Museums." In P. Vileneuve, ed., *From Periphery to Center: Art Museum Education in the 21st Century*, 31–40. Reston, VA: National Art Education Association, 2007.

Luke, J. J., A. Ong, and C. Figueiredo. *Research Brief #1: Who Uses Dedicated, Interactive Galleries in Art Museums, and Why Do They Use Them?* Technical research report. Edgewater, MD: Institute for Learning Innovation, 2011(a). www.artmuseumfamilyspaces.org.

———. *Research Brief #2: How Do Families Use Dedicated, Interactive Galleries in Art Museums?* Technical research report. Edgewater, MD: Institute for Learning Innovation, 2011(b). www.artmuseumfamilyspaces.org.

———. *Research Brief #3: What Do Parents Value about Dedicated Interactive Galleries in Art Museums?* Technical research report. Edgewater, MD: Institute for Learning Innovation, 2011(c). www.artmuseumfamilyspaces.org.

McManus, P. "Families in Museums." In R. Miles and L. Zavala, eds., *Towards the Museum of the Future: New European Perspectives*, 81–97. London: Routledge, 1994.

Moussouri, T. *Family Agenda—Family Learning*. Paper presented at the Visitor Studies Conference: Denver, Colorado, 1996.

———. "Negotiated agendas: Families in science and technology museums." *International Journal of Technology Management*, no. 25(5) (2003): 477–89.

Munley, M. E. *Early Learning in Museums: A Review of the Literature*. Smithsonian Institution, 2012. Accessed July 21, 2020, at https://www.si.edu/Content/SEEC/docs/mem%20literature%20review%20early%20learning%20in%20museums%20final%204%2012%202012.pdf.

Palmquist, S., and K. Crowley. "From Teachers to Testers: How Parents Talk to Novice and Expert Children in a Natural History Museum." *Science Education*, no. 91 (2007): 783–804.

Pattison, S. A., and L. Dierking. "Exploring Staff Facilitation that Supports Family Learning." *Journal of Museum Education*, 37(3) (2012): 69–80. Retrieved from http://informalscience.org/research/ic-000-000-007-379/Exploring_staff_facilitation.

Povis, K. T., and K. Crowley. "Family Learning in Object-Based Museums: The Role of Joint Attention." *Visitor Studies*, 18(2) (2015): 168–82. Retrieved from http://dx.doi.org/10.1080/10645578.2015.1079095.

Stein, J., and J. Luke. *Family Learning Project: Year 2 Evaluation* (unpublished evaluation report). Annapolis, MD: Institute for Learning Innovation, 2006.

Sterry, P. *An Insight into the Dynamics of Family Group Visitors to Cultural Tourism Destinations: Initiating the Research Agenda*. Paper presented at the New Zealand Tourism and Hospitality Research Conference, Wellington, New Zealand, 2004.

Wetterlund, K., and S. Sayre. 2003 Art Museum Education Programs Survey. Accessed November 2021: https://www.museum-ed.org/wp-content/uploads/2011/01/2003SurveyReportfinal.pdf.

Wolf, B., and E. Wood. "Integrating Scaffolding Experiences for the Youngest Visitors in Museums." *Journal of Museum Education*, no. 37(1) (2012): 29–38.

CHAPTER 2

Values Matter

ARE ART MUSEUMS ESSENTIAL TO FAMILIES?

FAMILIES ARE REGULAR AND EVEN FREQUENT VISItors to natural history museums, science centers, and, of course, children's museums. Art museums, however, attract the smallest percentage of the family audiences.[1] This finding suggests that art museums are less essential to families than other museums. To place art museums more prominently on a family's leisure-choice radar we need to better understand how the family audience values museums and, most importantly, the degree to which those values intersect with the broader leisure-time needs and interests of families in general.

Since non-art museums have a higher percentage of family visitors, it is not surprising that more research has been conducted on families in those museums. This also may have something to do with how much art museums value the family audience.[2] Each family arrives at a museum with a unique set of goals, motivations, and expectations for their museum visit. These desires, needs, and expectations are referred to by researchers as the "family agenda." Interestingly, a family's agenda at the museum has been shown to directly influence what they do during their visit and, more importantly, what benefits the group takes away.[3] Our thinking is that if a family continues to visit a museum with a similar agenda, then the benefits they derive from that visit are what they value about the visit.

Let's look at the ways in which family visitors have described the benefits from museums, in general, and art museums with interactive galleries, specifically. Keep in mind that the process of sorting all the ways in which visitors benefit from the museum experience can be tricky, primarily because these benefits are often interrelated. For families, the motivations to learn, interact socially, and enjoy themselves are so intricately intertwined that they essentially make up one agenda, and it is not a question of either-or.[4] Consequently, based on what families told researchers, we have created a more permeable illustration (figure 2.1) of the reasons families choose to visit museums,

which interestingly turned out to be the ways they told us they benefited from the experience. In short, what one comes in expecting is usually what one leaves with—assuming the museum did its job in addressing the visitor's agenda.

> Unlike in formal education, museums, archives and libraries will not be able to make judgments about how much their users have learnt or how much progress they have made. However, users themselves will be able to make judgments about their own learning. They will be able to articulate what they found out and if that was what they were looking for. They can say whether they were inspired or had an enjoyable time. Collecting evidence of learning outcomes in museums, archives and libraries therefore must involve asking users how they feel about their own learning.[5]

Fun in the Art Museum

> (The experiences we value most are those that) remove oneself from the everyday, creating opportunities to entertain each other and explore the environment visually, through sound, colors, or mood.
>
> —Parent, Frist Art Museum

When families are asked to describe what they find valuable about their museum experience, they often reference the fact that they enjoy themselves and have a good time. In a study of art museum interactive galleries, parents often assessed the quality of their experience according to how much their children enjoyed it.[6] Families in one interactive art space commented that their experience led them to believe that "museums can be fun."[7]

Stating fun or enjoyment as a learning outcome of a museum visit is sometimes balked at by art museum practitioners, particularly directors and curators, and sometimes by researchers. They counter that having fun is not an outcome, certainly not a learning outcome. Rather it is just a way that people might feel about the experience. Also, many people equate

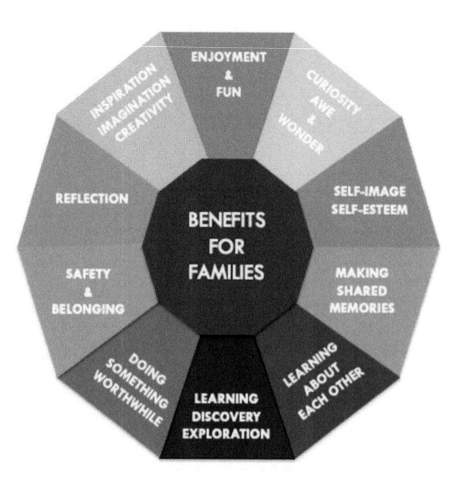

Figure 2.1. Research suggests that families benefit from the art museum visit in a variety of ways. Used by permission: Audience Focus Inc.

having fun with noise, running, or touching everything in sight. It is enough to make art curators feel quite faint. But if fun is what a family values, isn't that something we as practitioners should take to heart as we develop programs and our interactive spaces?

So, this resistance to fun as a learning outcome deserves attention. If families value the art museum experience because it was fun, for whatever reason, then their attitude toward the museum and perhaps toward art is likely to be more positive. One could argue that interactive spaces in art museums help to change many families' perceptions of art museums as being family unfriendly and elitist.[8] There are parents who do not perceive the art museum itself as a fun place to be, and consequently, the art museum does not appear much or at all on the leisure-time radar of these families. But we have the power to change this.

If a learning experience is associated with feelings of happiness and well-being, then it follows that whatever one counts as learning is more likely to be remembered, repeated, or expanded on. Political and economic researchers have begun to use happiness scales as one way to take the pulse of the population.[9]

Most importantly, art museum educators have begun to use the word "fun" in their descriptions of family programs. Perhaps labeling fun as a learning outcome, in its strictest sense, is a stretch, but it certainly is a *value* of the experience for families and parents to feel that the whole family benefits when they have had an enjoyable and worthwhile outing together.[10] This finding was even further strengthened in the FLING study. One parent in our study at the Frist Art Museum said she wanted to "encourage my children to have fun and not take life too seriously and to be happy."[11]

Part of what makes a museum visit fun for a family is that the experience is enjoyable for the whole family, children *and* adults. Parents often judge the success of family outings on the degree to which the experience is appropriate and appealing to everyone in the group. The interactive galleries in the FLING study were valued for how well they anticipated the needs and interests of all ages. A parent in the study at the High Museum of Art explained to us that the visits to the museum are "low maintenance, with something for everyone" and a place where her three children can interact with other children and be creative.[12]

Enjoyment can also mean that the museum experience gives the parents a break. The interactive galleries in the art museum allow parents to put aside their teacher, facilitator, or guide role and enjoy being a member of the family group because the teaching and guiding is already in place. As a parent at the Frist Art Museum put it: "I don't have to prepare, it's all there for me and I can enjoy being a mom and watch them learn as well as learn something new myself."[13] This quote highlights the important point that for the family the enjoyment also incorporates learning.

> I also wanted to know that somewhere in her childhood it was just fun.
>
> —Parent, High Museum of Art

Museum as a Place to Relax and Feel Safe

If identifying fun as a benefit of the art museum visit is difficult for museum staff to accept, a similar dilemma can be found in the research findings showing that families value museum experiences that allow them to feel relaxed and comfortable. Parents view family-oriented interactive spaces in art museums as physically and emotionally safe places for their children to play and explore. These parents say that one of the main benefits of participating in family-oriented events and activities is that their children develop a sense of ownership and belonging at the art museum.[14] Families often feel comfortable in these spaces because they don't have to worry about their children damaging art works (in the galleries) and do not feel the discomfort associated with being closely observed by security guards.[15]

In the LCS, parents continually mentioned how the interactive family galleries provided a place where everyone could relax and explore freely. It was the change of pace from the rest of the art museum that parents valued. Many parents admitted that they would not visit the art museum with their children as often, if at all, without the interactive gallery.[16]

When parents mentioned safety as a value of the interactive gallery, they meant both the physical and psychological safety of the space. This was particularly important for parents of young children and in families with two or more children. Considering things like how many doors are in the space and sightlines across the room really matters. That an attention to safety for all aged children was a conscious design decision in the interactive galleries was noted and appreciated by parents in the FLING study.[17] When parents referenced psychological safety issues, they usually referred to how welcoming the interactive spaces were or the degree to which the interactive spaces were a place where everyone in the family felt they belonged.

Self-Image and Self-Esteem

One value that might be surprising to think about in terms of the benefits of a museum visit is the impact it can have on how one feels about oneself. Museums can be places that positively affect one's self-image or sense of self-esteem. A study in UK art museums found that visiting the art museum with their grandchildren helps enhance the grandparent's positive self-image because it makes them feel younger and gives them something to look forward to.[18] Another study of families in Australian museums found a similar trend, noting that museum visits can lead to changes in the way visitors perceive themselves and their identity, and that in some cases, museums can help visitors to boost their confidence.[19] A study of families at a children's museum found that programs helped boost an individual's self-confidence and guided children in establishing "independence and autonomy."[20] Families often associate time spent with their children in an art museum with good parenting.[21] Parents feel that they are doing a good job when they take their children on worthwhile outings.

> It gives the children an opportunity to do things and to understand areas of art that I have basically no knowledge of. We cannot just do those things at home because I do not understand it and for them to be in a room where they see many different ways to do art and being able to participate in that is great.
>
> —Parent, Frist Art Museum

Creativity, Inspiration, and Imagination

Like self-esteem, a sense that one is a creative being cannot be taught as a skill, such as how to make a woodblock print can be taught. Rather, educators tend to assume that people are inherently capable and creative, only needing the proper environment in which to blossom. Although museum educators discuss the importance of encouraging creative and imaginative play while stimulating creativity and flexible thinking, the research data in this area was surprisingly scant.[22] Before our 2011 FLING study, we could find no studies that looked specifically at the relationship between interactive spaces in art museums and the effect on adult or child visitors' perceptions of themselves as creative beings. A few studies, along with our preliminary interviews for the FLING study, suggested that families liked interactive galleries because they believe these spaces stimulate their child's creative nature.[23]

> [The interactive space] really gives the children the chance to get into their imaginations and create their own worlds.
>
> —Parent, Speed Art Museum

Both the MUV and the LCS found that many parents were avid museum visitors before they had children, and when their children were born, they continued that practice gradually engaging their children in art making, art looking, and creative play. Parents perceived the most important benefits for their children when visiting interactive spaces in art museums were a positive increase in attitudes toward art and art museums and enhanced skills relative to art making. In fact, parents who were motivated to come to the museum because of the interactive space or for entertainment rated the benefits to children's art-making skills higher than did those parents who were motivated by the museum as a destination or a specific exhibition in the museum.[24]

> My son likes to draw. He looks at art and says: "Yes, I can do that." I don't want him to neglect that side of his development. There is more emphasis on sports and hunting and fishing and they can have a run with that, but I don't want the other side, the creative side, to be neglected.
>
> —Parent, High Museum of Art

In the LCS, parents continually mentioned the importance of the interactive spaces for stimulating and encouraging children's creativity. One family who began visiting the Frist Art Museum's Martin ArtQuest gallery when their daughter was very young, kept a large portfolio containing all of the artwork they created in the interactive gallery over the years. Another parent, who was visiting with her three children ages five, two, and a few months, vividly recalled discovering the Greene Family Learning Gallery at the High Museum of Art and thinking that it was "cool . . . I liked the open-ended play areas and the dress up and how the children could do whatever they wanted and draw things." On that same day, she purchased a membership to the High and the family has been attending frequently ever since.[25]

Parents identified shared values between the art museum interactive gallery and other leisure sites they frequented. This creativity benefit category was one of those crossover values. Parents often seek opportunities for their children to exercise the creative, imaginative muscles. Many of them say that this has become even more important because the arts are not as available in the schools as they once were.

Curiosity, Awe, and Wonder

As free-choice learning institutions, museums are best at stimulating curiosity and awakening visitors' sense of awe and wonder. Luke found that art museum visitors in London report feeling "fairly intense feelings of awe at some point during" their visit. She also found that awe was related to feelings of "curiosity, calm, inspiration, joy, and excitement."[26]

In a study of the Museum of Fine Art, Houston's education programs, parents rated stimulating curiosity and a sense of awe and wonder about art higher than any other learning or benefit.[27] Although learning something new and revisiting something already known were rated quite high, they were still lower than curiosity and awe. In that same study, we asked art museum educators in other art museums to guess what benefit their visitors would most frequently choose. Interestingly, practitioners rated learning something new as high as the visitors did but there was a large difference between their ratings of curiosity and awe. Where visitors rated curiosity and awe the highest, practitioners rated it quite low. Similarly, few museum practitioners mentioned stimulating curiosity as a goal or an outcome of their interactive space. How to interpret this difference between visitors' reported experience and practitioner's perception presents an interesting question. Did practitioners rate curiosity and awe low because they perceive that visitors did not receive these two benefits from their programs or do museum educators not have opportunities to witness visitors having their curiosity stimulated or experiencing awe and wonder?

It turns out that curiosity is more complex than one might think and might even be considered a key value of the museum visit. Susie Wilkening looked at the role of curiosity in museums[28] and found "the more we examine curiosity, the more important it appears to be, not only to individuals but to society." Her study found that the public in general (both museum visitors and nonvisitors) had a different concept of curiosity than academic researchers did. Although the general public understood curiosity to be "pursuing existing (deep) interests," researchers in the field of curiosity look at both deep *and* broad interests.

Researchers find that broad interests contribute more to that which is positive, helpful, and intended to promote social acceptance and friendship.

Wilkening's study then asked both those who did and did not attend museums: "what was their favorite outcome when their curiosity was sparked?" As you can see from figure 2.2, both museum visitors and nonvisitors were close in their selection of the outcome statement "learning more about things I am interested in." These results strongly support findings in other studies that museums are or should be in the business of curiosity stimulation because parents strongly value it for their children, as do museum visitors in general.

Discover, Explore, and Learn

> Our mindset is that every time you do something you learn something, and you just have to keep your eyes open to what that thing it is. The minute you stop learning is the minute you might just curl up and die. The way we look at it is that every day you learn something new.
>
> —Parent, High Museum of Art

It was not too long ago that learning in museums was most frequently defined as cognitive in nature. Many museum professionals felt that true learning occurred when visitors could recite the academic concepts or facts presented in an exhibition. Thankfully museum professionals have increasingly supported the idea that learning in museums needs to expand far beyond the traditional notion of learning as the acquisition of facts and skills to include a range of affective, perceptual, and social learning factors.[29]

Because museums are considered learning institutions, many parents view a museum visit as an opportunity to expose their children to history, science, and the arts. Families often say that they visit museums for educational purposes and to learn something new.[30] Most often, experiences that offer learning opportunities are likely to be valued by parents whose goals are to provide their children with a range of positive cultural experiences. We have found that adults and children do believe that they increase their knowledge, skills, understanding, and awareness of art as a result of their experience in the space.[31] Families also say they benefit from museum experiences that support exploration and discovery. Studies conducted in the Speed Art Museum's Art Sparks gallery and the Cincinnati Art Museum's Education Center found that parents highly value the fact that their children can explore using all of their senses and that they can discover art on their own.[32]

> Our motivation for visiting such varying sites was to do new things and expose the girls to various cultures.
>
> —Parent, Speed Art Museum

Our FLING case study found that parents valued the art museum interactive spaces because they provided a rich, sensory learning experience for their children to explore and discover.[33] Parents across all three museums in the study appreciated how the interactive spaces provided children with a wide variety of opportunities to learn through the senses. Certainly, this included hands-on experiences where children manipulated their environment, and it also included

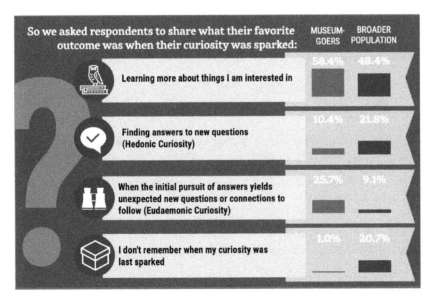

Figure 2.2. Comparison of museum visitors and the general public on favorite outcomes when curiosity is stimulated. Used by permission: Wilkening Consulting

learning through movement and sound or music. Because so many parents in our study had a long-term appreciation and love of the arts, they particularly valued the interactive spaces because they assisted them in instilling that same attitude in their children.

> I just like that they were exposed to a lot of stuff, all the time. And whether it is the more sophisticated art upstairs or more interactive things downstairs in Art Sparks, it's just that exposure. And they develop a love for culture. That's what I was after.
>
> —Parent, Speed Art Museum

The question whether museums, in general, and interactive spaces, in particular, should focus on education or entertainment is only an issue for museum practitioners. Visitors do not see a problem. It is both—fun *and* learning, or as they often put it, "having fun while learning." Remember, families choose to visit the museum in their limited leisure time. Why wouldn't they want both?

> We think about something that will be new. Trying to grow some new brain cells. That's the goal, I think, and so that they won't be afraid to try new things.
>
> —Parent, Speed Art Museum

Do Something Worthwhile

Whether you count "doing something worthwhile" as a valid learning outcome, it is a theme that frequently emerges for parents in art museums. Because most families come to the museum for their leisure time, it is fair for them to want that time spent together to be enjoyable—something that is not like school or work. Families definitely value the fun factor in interactive spaces, perceiving that learning is enhanced when everyone enjoys themselves. The important point is that parents do expect learning to happen; they just define learning differently than museums practitioners and researchers do. To be considered worthwhile, parents do not mean their children will learn facts such as three characteristics of Renaissance painting. It means that they and their children derive something that matters to them, something worth the time and money they spent. They want to explore and discover things on their own. They want to stand in awe of the work of humans that they never imagined could exist. They want to see and do extraordinary things—some-

thing they can't do somewhere else. That constitutes learning for the museum visitor.

Social Connection and Relationship Building

Many families state that their motivation for visiting the museum is to do something together as a family, a chance to bond, to have a shared experience. Consequently, it is not surprising that families frequently describe the value of the experience in terms of their social interaction. In general, families value museum experiences that allow them to interact with each other in meaningful ways. Parents often say that museum programs, events, and experiences geared toward families and children provide them with valuable opportunities to spend quality time with their children, develop shared memories, and strengthen family relationships.[34]

The FLING MUV study found that adults perceived interactive spaces in art museums to be highly valuable not just for their children or themselves as individuals but also to the parent-child relationship.[35] This is especially the case when parents' primary motivation for visiting the museums was entertainment or something fun to do. These parents felt that family bonding and memory-making were the most important benefit of the experience.

Parents reported that conversations on the ride home or at the dinner table were frequently fueled by their experiences at the art museum and the interactive spaces.[36] One parent said the greatest value of visiting the Speed Art Museum and Art Sparks gallery is that it increases the communication between her and her daughter.[37] She says:

> [One of the values] is definitely increased communication. I think when we're at home it is really easy for us to separate into our different areas of the house and do our own thing. So, I really like being able to dialogue with her more than I normally do.

Learning About Each Other

> Martin ArtQuest helps me to get to know my children. . . . I see what they enjoy. I love that it is something I get to do with them, not for them, but with them.
>
> —Parent, Frist Art Museum

Family members benefit by learning more about the personal interests and learning styles of individual members.[38] For example, a mother observing her preschool child painting in the style of Monet commented that she did not realize that his small motor skills were so developed and that he could now draw recognizable forms.

In a study of family programs at the USS Constitution Museum, families were invited to reflect on what they each learned about another family member and post their thoughts on a board (see figure 2.3). These programs encouraged families to work in teams to complete a task. Children often commented that their adult worked well as a teammate or that their adult was knowledgeable and a good builder. Children complimented their adult for having good ideas and said that they discovered their adult/parent was careful, quick, and awesome. Adults tended to remark on how their child had creative ideas and how the child was a good teammate or team motivator. They also remarked that their child was knowledgeable and even taught the adult something. Other qualities that adults noticed in their children were that they were good listeners, good boat builder, patient, and became more comfortable with their roles (assigned as part of the activity) as the program progressed.[39]

By going together as a family, we have that shared experience of being able to see the wonder in her eyes when she looks at something and to see her reaction to things. I really hope

Alex will experience the wonder and joy of other people's creativity.

—Parent, High Museum of Art

Similarly, grandparents highly value the time they spend with their grandchildren in the museum because they use that time to discover new information about each other and share stories that contribute to building the child's identity as a member of family group.[40] Evaluations of interactive spaces in art museums have similar findings. When asked, parents and caregivers say that they value opportunities for meaningful social experiences and that they use their time in the interactive galleries to build shared memories and develop meaningful relationships with each other.[41] For parents in the FLING study, one of the most valued benefits of the art museum interactive spaces was learning about their child's personal growth and development.[42]

Parents instinctively know their job is to grow fully functioning adults. They may not be able to articulate it that way but they frequently note their interest in situations where their children can practice social skills.[43]

At home, it was very easy for the family to fall into doing their own thing and the offsite visits help bring the family together.

—Parent, Speed Art Museum

Figure 2.3. Mother and son leaving sticky notes about what they learned about each other after a family program. Marianna Adams, Photographer, Used by permission: Audience Focus Inc.

Reflection

Visitors look at museums from a multifaceted lens of their life and experience. Parents go to great lengths to situate a family art museum experience within a larger context of the child's life. They look for opportunities to connect the art and interactive gallery activities with personal interests and the content of formal education lessons. Most families tend to strengthen these connections at home through family discussions, as well as through engaging in art-making activities inspired by their art museum and interactive gallery experience. So, we believe that for the families that use art museums as part of their lives, the museum is an essential component.

ARE FAMILIES ESSENTIAL TO ART MUSEUMS?

Is a strong and engaged family audience critical to an art museum's success in the twenty-first century? We believe it absolutely is. One way to tell if a museum is truly committed to serving families in a meaningful way is to first take a look at their website. Actions speak loudly. How easy is it to find information about visiting as a family with children? Does the museum offer programming for families—age appropriate, properly staffed, regular, times when families are available? Is space within the museum dedicated for families to use—a family gallery, classrooms, family labels or exhibitions, seating? What kind of family-friendly visitor services policies do they have—welcoming staff, strollers welcome or available, bottle feeding allowed? What creature comforts are provided—nursing rooms, family restrooms, kid friendly food in the café? The initial survey of art museum educators that we conducted at the beginning of the IMLS study in 2008 helped us understand where the field was twelve years ago regarding the status of families in art museums. In August 2020, we surveyed the field again to see what had or had not changed in terms of how art museums are, or are not, seeking to become essential to families.

Art Museums and Families—Then (2008)

As part of the preparation for the FLING research a survey was sent to the National Art Education Association's Museum Education division in 2008. Out of the eighty-six museums educators who completed the survey, more than half reported having a dedicated, family-oriented interactive space at their institution. The fact that 80 percent of the interactive spaces mentioned in this survey were younger than ten years old signaled to us that these types of spaces were a relatively new phenomenon. In fact, almost half were younger than five years old in 2008.

Museum educators were asked two different questions that sought information on benefits or outcomes for their interactive spaces. One question asked for three things they wanted the interactive space to accomplish. The second question asked for educators to list any outcomes that have been articulated for the space. We have found that, in general, it is difficult for museum educators to list outcomes or benefits for visitors. Instead, they tend to list broad goals or describe what they will do in the space (outputs) rather than how visitors benefit from it. Therefore, we were not surprised that these two questions did not receive a high number of responses,[44] and many of those responses were outputs and not benefits or outcomes. Of the responses that were outcomes, slightly less than half were in the category of "Fun & Creativity." The responses divided rather evenly between benefits in the "Fun & Creativity" and the "Discover & Learn" categories. Far fewer benefits referenced anything in the "Social & Quality Time" category.[45] Interestingly, "Curiosity" was specifically mentioned just once.

An overwhelming majority of museum educators emphasized that one of their primary goals or missions in developing interactive spaces was that visitors would be able to connect their experiences in the spaces to the collections and exhibitions in the rest of the museum. These educators hoped visitors would use the interactive spaces to make discoveries about the overall museum and explore exhibition themes and content.

We also asked how comfortable and welcoming educators felt their museum was to families. Many people talked about their interactive spaces as being places where families could relax and feel safe. One educator described their interactive space as a time-out spot for families to unwind. Overall, there was a strong desire among the responding museum educators to create spaces that were considered family friendly.

> If they haven't gotten to a museum as a kid, it's harder to create family cultural grounding. The Greene Family Learning Gallery is a place for families to feel comfortable and be welcome—to have age-appropriate activities that are available to them. For messaging to the public, it says, "we are family-friendly."
>
> —Patricia Rodewald, former Eleanor McDonald Storza Director of Education, High Museum of Art, Atlanta, Georgia

Another of the goals for museum educators was to tap into an audience segment that previously did not come—in almost all cases, this audience was families. Many museums were using their interactive spaces to dispel the image that art museums are static, dull, or family-unfriendly places to visit. We saw a desire among museum educators for visitors to have fun in the space and explore art through creative play and to express their own creativity. The answers to this question strongly illustrate how in 2008 the art museum education field was beginning to see the family audience as valuable and essential. We believe one of the reasons this was becoming a focus for museums in 2008 was the hope that having an interactive space or family-focused programming would increase overall attendance to the museum. In the same vein, museum educators hoped that changing the way the museum was perceived would encourage families to become repeat visitors or even members.

> You want them to know it is fun! That it is a hands-on experience and that they can be comfortable, welcomed and it is something special. The opportunity for a child to teach a parent and a parent to teach a child is invaluable.
>
> —Anne Henderson, Director of Education and Outreach, Frist Art Museum, Nashville, Tennessee

Art Museums and Families—Now (2018–2020)

In 2019, Colleen Dilenschneider published powerful data demonstrating that children who visited museums with their families grow up to feel more welcome at cultural organizations as adults than those who only visited as a child with school or other groups.[46] She found that "over 60% of adult visitors to museums and/or performing arts organizations first attended them as children" in family groups. It's not necessarily the cultural organization itself that makes a child into a lifelong lover of culture; it's also the memories families make together at that cultural organization. This revelation makes it even more important for art museums to take family audiences seriously. It's a matter of planning for future success. "This finding implies that engaging children is not only good for our missions to educate and inspire but may also help us cultivate our visitors and supporters of the future."[47] Investing in families is just good business!

> We know the museum can be a special place for families to learn together and create memories. We invest in family learning and resources because we

believe that early experiences with art and museum can shape positive attitudes and behaviors related to participation in culture. (2020, Nelson-Atkins Museum of Art)

The Crystal Bridges Museum of American Art conducted a study in 2018 that provided strong evidence for the value of the family audience to the art museum. They compared people visiting specifically for a family program with people coming for a typical day at the museum on a number of demographic measures. Family programs tend to attract more people who are local and connected in some way to the museum (see figure 2.4).[48] A local audience is an audience that can visit frequently, thereby providing a larger and more loyal visitor base.

LOCAL & CONNECTED

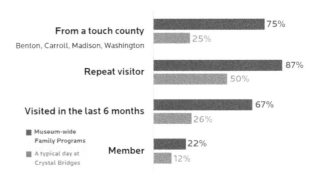

Figure 2.4. Family program guests are more likely to be local and connected to Crystal Bridges. Used by permission, Crystal Bridges Museum of American Art

In addition, family programs attract a more racially and ethnically diverse audience than we tend to see in the typical visitor (see figure 2.5).[49] Art museums that truly seek a more diverse audience are museums that sincerely value a range of programming and experiences for families.

In August 2020, we sent a new survey to leaders of learning and education departments in fifty-seven North American art museums. A total of thirty-one art museums participated in the study. Museums ranged from mid-size to large institutions that are located across the United States and one in Canada. The majority of respondents said family audiences are either a moderate or high priority at their museums.

All respondents reported that there have been major changes in how their organizations have approached, served, or valued family audiences within the past ten

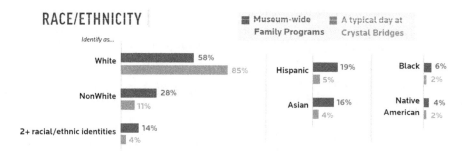

Figure 2.5. Family program guests are more likely to be racially and ethnically diverse. Used by permission, Crystal Bridges Museum of American Art

years. Most respondents reported major growth in how their museums serve family audiences, including:

1. Prioritizing families as an audience through targeted fundraising, outreach, and marketing, investments in new programs, resources, or spaces, and hiring new staff to support family audiences;
2. Growing the number of existing programs and experiences, services, or resources for family audiences;
3. Conducting more research and evaluation, prioritizing impact, being more responsive;
4. Expanding access to family audiences with the intent to be more inclusive; and
5. Creating more age-fluid experiences and resources to serve children of multiple ages and their adult caregivers simultaneously.

Although for some of these museums, families have been a priority audience for more than a decade, others noted that families have more recently become a higher-priority audience. Several museum educators said that by prioritizing families they are responding to their communities' needs, especially the need to provide life-enriching experiences for children and their parents and caregivers. Some of these organizations believe that providing family-based experiences, programs, and resources leads to greater diversity within their general visitor population, and many see it as a strategy to grow overall attendance and develop lifelong museumgoers. Almost all of the educators said their museums invest in family audiences by doing such things as raising funds for family-based programs and hiring staff to support family audiences.

Most educators said their museums currently provide a range of important amenities for family audiences, including family restrooms, family-focused orientation materials, and child-friendly food in the café. About half of these museums offer strollers or stroller parking and nursing rooms. A few museums offer family-based amenities or services, including free or no-cost admission or program offerings, child-focused merchandise in the museum store, and quiet "recharge" play spaces or sensory rooms. The few museums that do not provide any amenities for family audiences were university museums.

Programs continue to be the primary way art museums serve family audiences. All of the museums in this study said they provide programs that focus on encouraging intergenerational interaction. Most museums also provide family-friendly interpretation and special or dedicated web pages or online resources for families. Just more than half of the museums have dedicated family interactive spaces, while slightly less than half have dedicated interactive spaces or activities incorporated within their galleries or special exhibitions.

Of the museums that serve family audiences, all have dedicated staff or volunteers at their organizations that are responsible for implementing family experiences, such as leading family-oriented programs or tours, providing support in interactive spaces, or generally interacting with family audiences. Forty percent of educators said professional development on strategies to engage family audiences is provided for staff and volunteers at least two or more times per year. The other 60 percent said professional development is provided occasionally, once a year or less. Dedicated staff and professional development are good measures of the degree to which a museum "walks the talk." It is one thing to "say" that the family audience is important to the museum; it is another thing to actually provide the necessary support to convince families that they are important.

Programs targeting families, such as Free Family Festival Days, Family Mondays, Family Studios, and new virtual programming continue to receive stellar participation. We believe this is due to our commitment to providing exceptional experiences, investing in the same quality and consistency we'd pursue for adult programming. (Frist Art Museum)

Most museums have ongoing partnerships with local, family-focused organizations, and in just over half of the museums, families are mentioned in some way in their strategic plan, mission, or vision. More than half of the museums have conducted research or evaluation on family audiences and slightly less than half said their organizations have invited families to cocreate visitor experiences at the museum.

Looking Ahead

As we reviewed what the museum educators thought about the future, we were excited to see that many people thought that the way they serve family audiences in the next five years will continue to grow and change. Those changes include:

1. Increasing the number of dedicated spaces for families or programs and resources designed for family audiences;
2. Increasing virtual programs and resources that families can access at home;
3. Increasing access, equity, and inclusion;
4. Strategically planning to better serve families;
5. Increasing drop-in and on-demand resources over larger events and programs; and
6. Focusing on topics that address social issues, like racism, social justice, and health and well-being.

This new information indicates that the value of the family audience to the museum has begun to expand from the museum education department to all areas of the museum. It is our contention that if museums make families an essential audience, thoughtfully consider them in their planning, and invest in families through programming, marketing, and space allocations, the dividends can pay off for generations.

YOUR TURN

- With your team, consider what research tells us that parents value and what practitioners value and discuss why there might be a discrepancy. Take note that what families and museum professionals value are sometimes different.
- We as educators focus on the things we do and that's as it should be, but put as much if not more focus on *how* the visitor will benefit—from their perspective. Meet visitors where they are and consider what they value.

NOTES

1. A study with twelve museums in Balboa Park, San Diego, California, found that 57 percent of the total science and natural history museum attendance were family groups with children younger than age 18. History museums attracted 31 percent families, and art museums attracted 16 percent. (Adams, Renner, and Simpson, 2011).
2. See more about this in this chapter under the heading, Are Families Essential to Art Museums?
3. Dierking and Falk, 1994; Moussouri, 1996, 1997; Falk, Moussouri, and Coulson, 1998.
4. Falk and Dierking, 1992; Ellenbogen, 2002; Kelly, Savage, Griffin, and Tonkin, 2004.
5. Hooper-Greenhill, Dodd, and Moussouri, 2003, 10.
6. Adams, 1999.
7. Adams, Moreno, Polk, and Buck, 2003.
8. Adams and Moussouri, 2002.
9. Graham, 2010.
10. Although different academic disciplines often use the terms "value," "benefit," and "outcomes" in specific ways, for our purposes we use them interchangeably. You will notice that we use the terms "value" and "benefit" more often because "outcome" evolved from a formal, school-based environment. Because a museum visit is a free-choice or leisure-learning experience and people come for vastly different reasons than they have for attending school, we tend to prefer the terms "benefit" and "value."
11. Adams and Ancelet, 2011.
12. Ibid.
13. Ibid.
14. Stein and Luke, 2006; Adams, 1999; Durbin, 2002; Hood, 1989.
15. Williams, 2005.
16. Adams and Ancelet, 2011.
17. Ibid.
18. Beaumont and Sterry, 2005.
19. Kelly, et al., 2004.
20. Luke, Cohen Jones, Dierking, Adams, and Falk, 2002, 15.
21. Adams, 1999; Kelly, et al., 2004; Sterry and Beaumont, 2006.
22. Forbes, Hill, and Adams, 2005.
23. Adams, Luke, and Ancelet, 2008.
24. Luke, Ong, and Figueiredo, 2011(a), 2011(c); Adams and Ancelet, 2011.
25. Adams and Ancelet, 2011.
26. Luke, 2021, 47.
27. Adams, et al., 2008.
28. Wilkening Consulting, 2020.
29. Dierking and Falk, 1994; Dierking, Luke, and Falk, 2002; Adams, et al., 2008; Stein and Luke, 2006; Luke and Adams, 2007; Taylor, 2006; Hooper-Greenhill, et al., 2003.

30. Dierking, 1989; Ellenbogen, 2002, 2003; Hilke, 1989; Laetsch, Diamond, Gottfried, and Rosenfeld, 1980; Moussouri, 1996, 1997, 2003; Edwards, 2005.
31. Adams, 1999; Beaumont and Sterry, 2005; Kelly, et al., 2004.
32. Adams, 1999; Stein and Luke, 2006.
33. Adams and Ancelet, 2011.
34. Borun, et al., 1998; Dierking, et al., 2002; Kelly, et al., 2004.
35. Luke, Ong, and Figueiredo, 2011(c).
36. Luke, et al., 2011(c); Adams and Ancelet, 2011.
37. Adams and Ancelet, 2011.
38. Luke, et al., 2002; Luke, Tomczuk, Foutz, et al., 2019; Letourneau, Meisner, Neuwirth, and Sobel, 2017.
39. Adams, 2015.
40. Beaumont and Sterry, 2005; Kelly, et al., 2004.
41. Adams, 1999; Beaumont and Sterry, 2005; Borun, et al., 1998; Stein and Luke, 2006.
42. Luke, et al., 2011(a), (b), (c).
43. Adams and Ancelet, 2011.
44. A total of fifty out of eighty-six people responded to the question "What are 3 things your museum wanted to accomplish by developing such an interactive space?" and ten out of eighty-six people responded to the prompt "If your interactive gallery or space has clearly articulated visitor outcomes, please describe them."
45. The breakdown was: 47 percent "Fun & Creativity," 47 percent "Discover & Learn," and 11 percent "Social & Quality Time." Percentages total more than 100% because survey respondents could reference more than one benefit category.
46. Dilenschneider, 2019.
47. Ibid.
48. Goss, 2018.
49. Ibid.

REFERENCES

Adams, M. *Family Programs Evaluation: USS Constitution Museum* (unpublished technical report). Audience Focus, 2015.

———. *Summative Evaluation Report of the Art Learning Center Art Sparks Interactive Gallery, Speed Art Museum, Louisville, KY* (unpublished evaluation report). Annapolis, MD: Institute for Learning Innovation, 1999.

Adams, M., and J. Ancelet. *Longitudinal Case Study Summaries*. 2011. Accessed October 28, 2020, at www.artmuseumfamilyspaces.org.

Adams, M., J. Luke, and J. Ancelet. *What We Do and Do Not Know about Family Learning in Art Museum Interactive Spaces: A Literature Review*. 2008. Accessed October 28, 2020, at www.artmuseumfamilyspaces.org.

Adams, M., C. Moreno, M. Polk, and L. Buck. "The Dilemma of Interactive Art Museum Spaces." *Art Education: The Journal of the National Art Education Association*, no. 56(5) (2003): 42–52.

Adams, M., and T. Moussouri. *The Interactive Experience: Linking Research and Practice*. Paper presented at Interactive Learning in Museums of Art and Design symposium, London, UK, May 17–18, 2002.

Adams, M., N. Renner, and P. Simpson. *Evaluating Balboa Park Experiences: 2010 Collaborative Audience Research Study—Cross-Museum Report* (unpublished research report). Annapolis, MD: Audience Focus Inc., 2011.

Adams, M., B. Schneider, J. Ancelet, R. Gavounas, and V. Ramirez. *Museum of Fine Arts Houston A Place for All People & Gateway to Art Evaluation of Community Partnerships & Museum Learning A Wallace Foundation Project* (unpublished technical report). Audience Focus Inc., 2008.

Beaumont, E., and P. Sterry. "A Study of Grandparents and Grandchildren as Visitors to Museums and Art Galleries in the UK." *Museums and Society*, no. 3(3) (2005): 167–80.

Borun, M., J. Dritsas, J. I. Johnson, et al. *Family Learning in Museums: The PISEC Perspective*. Philadelphia, PA: The Franklin Institute, 1998.

Dierking, L. "The Family Museum Experience: Implications from Research." *Journal of Museum Education*, no. 14(2) (1989): 9–11.

Dierking, L., and J. Falk. "Family Behavior and Learning in Informal Science Settings: A Review of the Research." *Science Education*, no. 78(1) (1994): 57–72.

Dierking, L., J. Luke, and J. Falk. *The Children's Museum of Indianapolis: Family Learning Initiative* (unpublished evaluation report). Annapolis, MD: Institute for Learning Innovation, 2002.

Dilenschneider, C. "*School Groups vs. Family Visitors: Which Kids Come Back as Adults? (DATA)*." Know Your Own Bone blog. September 2019. Accessed October 10, 2020, at https://www.colleendilen.com/2019/09/04/school-group-vs-family-visitors-which-kids-come-back-as-adults-data/.

Durbin, G. *Interactive Learning in the British Galleries, 1500–1900*. Paper presented at Interactive Learning in Museums of Art and Design Symposium, London, UK. May 17–18, 2002.

Edwards, R. *The Getty Family Room: Unpacking the Ideas and Assumptions behind the Development of an Interactive Space*. Paper presented at the J. Paul Getty Museum Symposium, "From Content to Play: Family-Oriented Interactive Spaces in Art and History Museums," Los Angeles, California, June 4–5, 2005. Accessed October 30, 2020, at http://www.getty.edu/education/symposium/Edwards.pdf.

Ellenbogen, K. *From Dioramas to the Dinner Table: An Ethnographic Case Study of the Role of Science Museums in Family Life*. (Dissertations Abstracts International, 64(03), 846A. University Microfilms No. AAT30-85758) 2003.

Ellenbogen, K. M. "Museums in Family Life: An Ethnographic Case Study." In Leinhardt, Crowley, and Knutson, eds., *Learning Conversations in Museums*, 81–101. Mahwah, NJ: Lawrence Erlbaum Associates, Inc., 2002.

Falk, J., and L. Dierking. *The Museum Experience*. Washington, DC: Whalesback Books, 1992.

Falk, J., T. Moussouri, and D. Coulson. "The Effect of Visitors' Agendas on Museum Learning." *Curator*, no. 41 (1998): 107–20.

Forbes, J., K. Hill, and M. Adams. *Understanding Audiences: The Creation of the High Museum of Art Family Learning Gallery*. Paper presented at the J. Paul Getty Museum Symposium, "From Content to Play: Family-Oriented Interactive Spaces in Art and History Museums," Los Angeles, California, June 4–5, 2005. Accessed October 30, 2020, at http://www.getty.edu/education/symposium/Forbes.pdf.

Goss, J. *Museum-Wide Family Programs vs. a Typical Day at Crystal Bridges*. Unpublished technical report. Bentonville, AR: Crystal Bridges Museum of American Art, 2018.

Graham, C. "The Economics of Happiness." *Washington Post*. January 3, 2010. Accessed October 30, 2020, at http://www.washingtonpost.com/wp-dyn/content/article/2009/12/31/AR2009123101153.html.

Hilke, D. D. "The Family as a Learning System: An Observational Study of Families in Museums." In B. Butler and M. Sussman, eds. *Museum Visits and Activities for Family Life Enrichment*, 101–27. London: Hayworth Press, 1989.

Hood, M. "Leisure Criteria of Family Participation and Nonparticipation in Museums." *Marriage and Family Review*, no. 13(2) (1989): 151–70.

Hooper-Greenhill, E., J. Dodd, and T. Moussouri. *Measuring the Outcomes and Impact of Learning in Museums, Archives and Libraries: The Learning Impact Research Project*. Leicester: Research Centre for Museums and Galleries, 2003.

Kelly, L., G. Savage, J. Griffin, and S. Tonkin. *Knowledge Quest: Australian Families Visit Museums*. Sydney: Australian Museum & the National Museum of Australia, 2004.

Laetsch, W., J. Diamond, J. Gottfried, and S. Rosenfeld. "Children and Family Groups in Science Centers." *Science and Children*, no. 17(6) (1980): 14–17.

Letourneau, S. M., R. Meisner, J. L. Neuwirth, and D. M. Sobel. "What Do Caregivers Notice and Value about How Children Learn through Play in a Children's Museum?" *Journal of Museum Education*, 42(1) (2017): 87–98.

Luke, J. J. "'The Bloody Hell and Holy Cow Moment': Feeling Awe in the Art Museum." *Curator: The Museum Journal*, 64(2) (2021): 41–55.

Luke, J. J., and M. Adams. "What Research Says about Learning in Art Museums." In P. Vileneuve, ed., *From Periphery to Center: Art Museum Education in the 21st Century*, 31–40. Reston, VA: National Art Education Association, 2007.

Luke, J. J., M. Cohen Jones, L. Dierking, M. Adams, and J. Falk. *The Children's Museum of Indianapolis Family Learning Initiative: Phase II Programs Study* (unpublished research report). Annapolis, MD: Institute for Learning Innovation, 2002.

Luke, J. J., A. Ong and C. Figueiredo. *Research Brief #1: Who Uses Dedicated, Interactive Galleries in Art Museums, and Why Do They Use Them?* Technical research report. Edgewater, MD: Institute for Learning Innovation, 2011(a). www.artmuseumfamilyspaces.org.

——. *Research Brief #2: How Do Families Use Dedicated, Interactive Galleries in Art Museums?* Technical research report. Edgewater, MD: Institute for Learning Innovation, 2011(b). www.artmuseumfamilyspaces.org.

——. *Research Brief #3: What Do Parents Value about Dedicated Interactive Galleries in Art Museums?* Technical research report. Edgewater, MD: Institute for Learning Innovation, 2011(c). www.artmuseumfamilyspaces.org.

Luke, J. J., E. D. Tomczuk, S. Foutz, et al. "What Caregivers Observe about Their Children's Learning During a Visit to the Children's Museum." *Journal of Museum Education*, no. 44(4) (2019): 427–38.

Moussouri, T. *Family Agenda—Family Learning*. Paper presented at the Visitor Studies Conference, Denver, Colorado, 1996.

——. *Family Agendas and Family Learning in Hands-On Museums*. Doctoral dissertation. University of Leicester, Leicester, UK, 1997.

——. "Negotiated Agendas: Families in Science and Technology Museums." *International Journal of Technology Management*, no. 25(5) (2003): 477–89.

Philadelphia-Camden Informal Science Education Collaborative. *Family Learning in Museums: The PISEC Perspective*. Philadelphia: The Franklin Institute, 1998.

Stein, J., and J. Luke. *Family Learning Project: Year 2 Evaluation* (unpublished evaluation report). Annapolis, MD: Institute for Learning Innovation, 2006.

Sterry, P., and E. Beaumont. "Methods for Studying Family Visitors in Art Museums: A Cross-disciplinary Review of Current Research." *Museum Management and Curatorship*, no. 21 (2006): 222–39.

Taylor, B., ed. *Inspiring Learning in Galleries*. London: Engage, 2006.

Williams, P. *Family Spaces and Activities*. Paper presented at the J. Paul Getty Museum Symposium, "From Content to Play: Family-Oriented Interactive Spaces in Art and History Museums," Los Angeles, California, June 4–5, 2005. Accessed October 30, 2020, at http://www.getty.edu/education/symposium/Williams.pdf.

Wilkening Consulting. *Data Stories: Infographics That Tell a Story, Curiosity: A Primer* (2020 Annual Survey of Museum-Goers: Data Story #3. 2020. Accessed October 26, 2020, at http://www.wilkeningconsulting.com/data-stories.html.

CHAPTER 3

Stop, Look, Listen

PICTURE A MOTHER AND TWO CHILDREN, A GIRL, AGE eight, and a boy, age ten, walking through an art museum on their way to a family interactive gallery. The mother momentarily stops to talk to a museum staff member, and the children quietly wander over to look at a large contemporary sculpture nearby. Their behavior is quite proper, and they appear to enjoy themselves, laughing, pointing, and even mimicking the gestures in the sculpture with their bodies. The mother notices the children have moved away from her, and a bit startled, she calls to them, saying, "Oh no, this isn't your area of the museum, come, we are going there now," and the family moves quickly, passing, but not looking at, the art objects on their way to the family gallery.

When we witnessed this small interchange at an art museum, our hearts broke. This incident caused our group of museum educators and museum researchers to ask some questions we probably should have been asking years earlier. We wondered how many parents shared this mother's perspective. Given that many museum educators designed their interactive family galleries to be launch pads where families are inspired to visit the museum proper, we thought it might be wise to become more curious about how families actually used the art museum and the interactive spaces.

TIME SPENT

We started by looking at what research had to say about how much time family groups spent in all types of museums, and we saw a general pattern across museums. Repeatedly, studies found that family groups, as well as all adult visitors, tended to spend an average of two hours on their museum visit.[1] There are certainly wide variations from a visit a few minutes long to one lasting most of a day. Of course, the amount of time spent can also vary depending on the size of a museum or on idiosyncratic family needs, such as a child becoming overtired. But the average seemed to stay fairly steady across museums at two hours.

Although a valuable piece of information, time spent tells us little of the story of how families use the museum.

GENERAL PATTERNS OF USE

Our next area of inquiry was to investigate what families actually did in the art museum to determine any patterns that emerged across families and museums. Once families make the decision to visit the museum, they tend to follow a fairly predictable pattern and routine. This pattern usually begins with a three- to ten-minute orientation period, followed by fifteen to forty-five minutes of intensive exhibition viewing and an almost equal twenty to forty minutes of exhibition cruising, ending with a three- to ten-minute leave-taking period.[2] Families tend to divide their attention among exhibits, the museum setting as a whole, and their own social group.

The majority of a family's attention is focused on exhibit viewing, which, toward the beginning of the visit, is conducted in an orderly and concentrated manner and then becomes less systematic, somewhat faster, and more opportunistic as the visit progresses. Family visitors' attention toward social interaction is less than what they exert toward exhibit viewing, but the focus on social interactions tends to remain consistent throughout the visit, although the quality of the social interaction may degrade somewhat as fatigue sets in.[3] Interestingly, social interactions with people outside of the family group, such as other visitors or museum staff, tend to occur more toward the end of the visit. Families in a science museum on average spend about 80 percent of their time in exhibit areas, with the remaining time split among the café, museum store, restrooms, or waiting areas.[4]

Tracking where families go in the museum takes a great deal of time and is usually out of the scope of most evaluation projects. Some research shows that families plan for an extended break in their museum visit, and our FLING LCS found the same pattern.[5] This break usually occurs about halfway through a museum visit, and families use this time to eat a packed lunch or sit at the café or engage in activities that might not be appropriate for exhibition spaces, such as coloring, playing with toys, or "playful wrestling."[6] Parents may even take children outside the museum or into a play space so that they can let off steam. This type of visit behavior is both for the benefit of the children, who need to release energy, and for the parents, who need "time out from the demands of close supervision."[7]

Most family visits in the art museum include time in the collections or exhibitions, usually covering two to three galleries or areas of the museums. Families spend about 40 percent of their time in the interactive galleries and the rest of their time was in the collections or exhibitions, at programs, in the café, or shop.[8]

For most of the observed visits in our LCS, the social group tended to include the mother with children but occasionally included the father. Mothers noted that this was usually their visit pattern because they tended to visit during times when the father was working. For many families, particularly those who home school, the art museum visit was a wider social experience because they frequently met other home school families. Food was also a part of the overall experience for most families. They talked about it, ate at a restaurant, or brought their own food for eating during or after the visit.[9]

Membership in the art museum also had an impact on how families structured their visit. Member families tended to visit fewer galleries than nonmembers. Members were also more likely to participate in family programs than nonmember families. When families were members of other museums, but not the museum in the study, they were more likely to only visit the interactive space.[10]

Previous museum visitation patterns or familiarity with the institution also had an impact on the visit. Families who frequently visited zoos, aquariums, or science centers did fewer things in the art museum and went to fewer galleries. Families who frequently visited art and history museums, in general, tended to do more things in the museum and go to more galleries and were least likely to make the interactive space their only stop. Families who frequently went to children's museums went to more family programs in the art museum.[11]

Another factor that impacted how families connected with the art museum and its interactive gallery was their personal interest in art. Parents or caregivers who said they were more interested in art tended to do more things in the art museum and visit more galleries. A high interest in art meant the interactive space was also more likely to be the middle or last stop. Those with a low interest in art tended to make the interactive space their only stop.[12]

By going together as a family, we have that shared experience of being able to see the wonder in her eyes when she looks at something and to see her reaction to things. I really hope Alex will experience the wonder and joy of other people's creativity.

—Parent, High Museum of Art

Although these interactive spaces are primarily focused on the family audience, what about school groups and adults? In some cases, the family interactive gallery is also designed to be used by school groups. Usually, a large student group is broken into smaller groups of ten to fifteen students per docent or museum teacher and rotated around the museum with the interactive gallery being one of the stops on their visit. There are no right answers here, but your decision has important design and staffing implications. Both the Frist's Martin ArtQuest and the Speed's ArtSparks spaces were designed to accommodate school groups. These two spaces were also fully monitored by paid staff during all open hours.

The Frist's Martin ArtQuest redesign in 2018 kept larger groups in mind. The art stations are designed for groups to collaborate on projects. Three to four students can work together at the loom station or to create an animation video together. The philosophy behind the redesign supports twenty-first-century learning skills—collaboration, creativity, and communication. Martin ArtQuest activities are typically connected to the exhibitions targeted for K–12 visitors. The activities complement or enhance the main concepts in the exhibition and offer each visitor, whether individual or group, the opportunity to achieve a depth of immersion and personal satisfaction. Activities are designed to be highly repeatable, no matter how frequently visitors attend.

On the other hand, the High's Greene Family Learning Gallery was designed only for the drop-in family audience. School or camp groups were not allowed to visit. The ninth Greene Family Learning Gallery (2005–2018) was smaller than the Frist and Speed spaces, but more importantly, the space was not staffed. When an interactive space is used by groups of children, the wear and tear is significantly increased and needs to be constantly monitored by staff. Even though the tenth version of the Greene Family Learning Gallery doubled in square footage, it is still closed to school or camp groups. High staff do make regular rounds in the space, but there is not a constant staff presence.

We could not find any published studies of how school groups use art museum interactive spaces, yet there is a wealth of data on how all types of audiences, including school groups, use interactive stations in science and children's museums. The Frist Art Museum staff looked closely at that research and best practices in science and children's museums, learning from how they worked with larger school groups. In 1999 a summative study was conducted in the Speed's ArtSparks gallery that collected data on the family and school audience.[13] In particular, this study sought to understand the differences in the ways family and school audiences used the space and the relationship of the ArtSparks experience to their experiences in the permanent collection. The study of the school audience also focused on ways schoolteachers and museum docents perceived of and used ArtSparks as a teaching resource.

Specifically, there was some concern among museum staff that ArtSparks might be so much fun that the rest of the museum would feel dull in comparison. For those students who had never visited the Speed before, this was apparently the case. ArtSparks was a different and largely unexpected experience for these new student visitors. It is therefore not surprising that it figured more prominently in their memories a few weeks after their visit to the Speed. On the other hand, students who had previously visited the Speed and ArtSparks tended to remember as much from the permanent collection as from the interactive gallery. ArtSparks appeared to provide students with a stronger framework for looking at and thinking about the art collections.

For the High's ninth family space, the design (colors and finishes) tended to communicate that it was for fairly young children. This was an intentional design choice by the High staff. Adults were allowed in the space, of course, and some would wander in to see what was happening, but they rarely stayed long. The High staff made a conscious design shift in the tenth Greene Family Learning Gallery (2018 to present). The space visually communicates elegant *and* child friendly, but tells visitors it is not just for kids. This approach clearly worked as is so delightfully expressed by the Instagram post in figure 3.1 showing a couple visiting the High's Greene Family Learning Gallery.

Patterns in the Art Museum Collections and Special Exhibitions

Given that many museum educators initially designed family interactive galleries to encourage fami-

Figure 3.1. Adults in the High's Greene Family Learning Gallery for "Friday evening shenanigans." Retrieved from #HighMuseum Instagram post; Used by permission from Instagram poster Keyine

lies to visit the permanent collections and special exhibitions,[14] we realized we needed to know more about how families used these resources in the art museum. Parents in the case studies felt that visiting the museum collections or exhibitions was an important component of their family outing, and almost all of the visits included time in the art galleries.[15]

At the same time, parents recognized that many children found it difficult to stay attentive for very long while looking at art, so most visits to the art galleries were parent-initiated and -driven. Consequently, they became quite creative in the strategies they employed to focus children and help them learn to engage in looking more thoughtfully and carefully.[16]

Typically, family groups stayed fairly close together while in the art galleries. Families with older children were more likely to engage in a social group pattern of wandering a few feet away from each other, looking on their own, then drawing back together. It was common to observe parents engaging their children by reading a label out loud and then asking a few questions to engage the child in conversation about the art. Parents tended to initiate discussions in an organic way, not forcing conversation but stimulating and facilitating thoughtful reflection as the teachable moment arose. Some parents created their own "games" on the spot, typically an "I spy" search-and-find type of activity. A few mothers made up scavenger hunts. One mother always visited the new exhibitions on her own or with a friend before taking her child back to the museum because she wanted to be sure her daughter would enjoy the experience. Another family with older children engaged them successfully in an exhibition by getting the audio guides that, the father reported, made his boys "feel grown up."[17]

> I think it's been interesting to watch that sort of graduation from Art Sparks into the other realms—like when I took the girls to the Native American exhibit and they did the scavenger hunt. It was Ellie and her friend Leah, and they had such a good time going upstairs to the upper galleries.
>
> —Parent, Speed Art Museum

Patterns in the Interactive Family Galleries

In contrast to the ways adults and children interact in the galleries, in the interactive spaces, parenting styles varied from active facilitation to a more "hands-off" approach of watchful noninterference, remaining available to answer questions and offer encouragement. Parents said that the interactive space provided children with an opportunity to "blow off steam" created while following stricter behavior rules in the art galleries. For families with young children, the interactive spaces provided a psychologically and physically safe place for children to explore and discover on their own and a sensory-rich environment that supported early learning development. Some parents described the spaces as a kind of anchor in their art museum visit. Without the interactive spaces, some parents said they would not come to the museum as often or even at all.[18]

The interactive gallery provided freedom for children—freedom to explore and engage in creative play, together or independently. Older or more self-directed children tended to choose their own activity. Families with one child tended to stay together in the interactive gallery, at least for part of the visit. Sometimes these families engaged in a type of "parallel play" with each family member engaged in their own activity but talking to each other and often showing each other their work.

RELATIONSHIP OF INTERACTIVE GALLERY TO THE LARGER MUSEUM VISIT

For the LCS in the FLING research, we created a coding rubric of learning behaviors we observed in the galleries and other sites where we accompanied the families. The learning behaviors were adapted from Bloom's Cognitive and Affective Taxonomy.[19] See figure 3.2 for more details on how we articulated the

Learning Behaviors

Figure 3.2. Chart of categories of observed family learning behaviors adapted from Bloom's Taxonomy. Used by permission: Audience Focus Inc.

ANALYZE
Categorize, Compare-Contrast, Differentiate, Identify, Illustrate, Generalize

ATTEND
Support, Listen, Remember, Observe, Select, Confirm, Correct, Praise, Focus, Touch, Point

CREATE
Combine, Multiple Points of View, Build, Design, Invent, Synthesize, Adapt, Hypothesize, Experiment, Pretend, Imagine, Perform

APPLY
Explain, Invite, Propose, Demonstrate, Discuss, Practice, Write, Value, Appreciate

CHARACTERIZE
Debate, Evaluate, Conclude, Solve, Summarize, Compromise, Reflect

UNDERSTAND
Interpret, Respond, Participate, Describe, Read, Spell, Instruct, Define, Imitate

museum learning behaviors. Keep in mind that these are descriptions of behaviors that are associated with learning across multiple studies. They do not describe *what* is learned. We coded the observations (six visits per family, six families in three museums for a total of 108 observations, about half in the art museum and half in another site chosen by the family that shared at least one characteristic with the art museum experience. Then we compared how often families engaged in these learning behaviors in the art museum galleries and the interactive spaces. See figure 3.3.

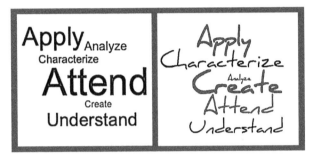

Figure 3.3. WordCloud comparison of family learning behaviors. Left: Family learning behaviors in art museum galleries. Right: Learning behaviors in family interactive spaces in art museums. Used by permission: Audience Focus Inc.

Unsurprisingly, the most frequent family learning behavior in the art museum collections and exhibitions was in the "Attend" category, specifically, observing and pointing at art with some remembering (e.g., the child or adult referenced a shared memory that was piqued by the art). The next most frequent learning behavior was in the "Apply" category, which included explaining something and inviting someone to see or do something with them. The learning behavior category of "Understand" was next, reading, describing, and interpreting—all behaviors one expects to see in an art museum. The behavioral categories of "Analyze" and "Characterize" were not often observed among the families in our study. Understandably, there were very few incidents of behaviors in the "Create" category.[20]

As might be expected in an interactive space where families are encouraged to manipulate, express, and create, patterns of learning behaviors were different from those in the galleries that contain works of art. The strongest learning behavior categories in interactive spaces were "Create," such as build, design, experiment, pretend, imagine, or perform, and the category of "Apply," including propose an activity or solution, discuss, practice, or demonstrate. Of the four remain-

ing categories of behavior three were quite strong (Characterize, Attend, and Understand), while there was scant evidence of behaviors around "Analyze." In contrast to the adult-child interaction in the art galleries where adults initiated most learning behaviors, children initiated more if not most of these learning behaviors when in the interactive spaces.[21]

Articulating the relationship of the interactive space with the art in the collections and exhibitions was not an easy thing for parents to do. One child expressed this connection most succinctly when he used a metaphor of "cheese and crackers" to express how he experiences the relationship between the art galleries and interactive space. He explained how you have "all the boring stuff [galleries] and then all the good stuff [Interactive Gallery]," but both are important and go together; "they aren't really good alone, but they go great together."[22]

An important question for our group of museum educators and researchers to explore was "when, during an art museum visit, do families visit the interactive gallery?" Obviously the location of the interactive gallery in the museum has an effect on when it is visited but the answer is a bit more nuanced. The large-scale MUV study #2 was the most effective at gathering data on when families visited the interactive galleries. Figure 3.4 illustrates that across the three museums in the FLING study, the largest segment of visitors stopped at the interactive galleries at the end of their visit.[23] Family visitors at the Speed Art Museum were more likely than those at the other two museums to make the interactive gallery the only stop on the museum visit with 34 percent of the visitors making this choice compared to only 4 percent of High Museum of Art family visitors. Speed Art Museum visitors were also less likely to make the interactive gallery the last stop as 20 percent of families went to ArtSparks last, compared to between 40 percent and 50 percent of visitors at the High and Frist museums.[24]

The Interactive Gallery Is the Only Place Visited

In six of forty-nine observed case study visits in the art museums, families did not go into the art galleries but confined their time to the interactive gallery only. One mother explained that she did not take her four children into the art galleries because she felt they were just too young, and it would be difficult for her to manage them there. As they grew older, her goal was to gradually introduce the gallery experience to the children.[25]

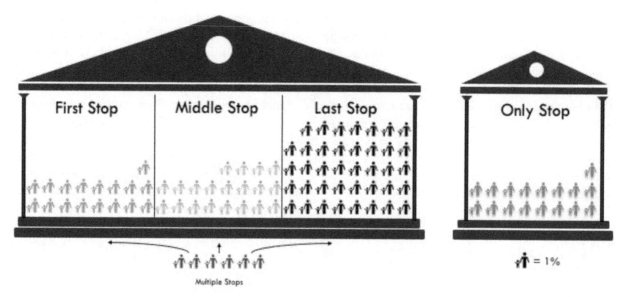

First Stop   Middle Stop   Last Stop   Only Stop

Multiple Stops

👤 = 1%

Figure 3.4.   Families tend to visit the interactive galleries at the end of their visit. Used by permission: Audience Focus Inc.

I am not going to expect my four-year-old daughter to appreciate American art and this statue or the sculptures and some of the paintings. I don't expect her to have an appreciation but as far as the Greene Family Learning Gallery even though you are not necessarily looking at a sculpture, she [daughter] has her own ability to create and explore in there using the blocks or the magnetic wall or using her imagination by using the fabrics to pretend.

—Parent, High Museum of Art

For example, the Shelburne family (figure 3.5) made their first visit to the Speed Art Museum in 2002, when the children, Ares and Athena, were just two years and a few months old, respectively.[26] Hera, the mother, explained that the combination of just "wanting to get out" and being a practicing artist prompted her to take the children to the Speed Museum. From the very first visit, they became frequent visitors. Hera says they came often because it was "guaranteed fun for the children."

During the LCS when Ares and Athena were ages ten and eight, respectively, the family only visited Art Sparks on two of the three observed visits. When the children visited with their father, Zeus, the pattern followed an alternation between creating and playing individually and creating and playing together. In general, both children were likely to approach or join an activity and then leave it quickly, flittering from one exhibit to the next. Athena was slightly more likely to follow this pattern than her brother,

who at times sat and focused on an activity, whether it was drawing, building, or painting. Both children appeared to enjoy pretending and using their imaginations and were often observed making up stories and enacting imaginary scenes. When deciding what to see and do, both children made suggestions, which in most instances were accepted and agreed on by the group. Socially, the children spent more time interacting with each other or other children than with their parents. In most instances, Hera and Zeus tended to observe their children rather than engage directly, offering suggestions and feedback when needed or requested. On a few occasions, Zeus or Hera joined in and directly participated in an activity; however, this happened less frequently. Neither Ares nor Athena

Figure 3.5.   Family members engaged in art-making activity at the Speed Art Museum Art Sparks Gallery, Louisville, Kentucky. Used by permission: Marianna Adams, Photographer

seemed to be shy about interacting with other children in Art Sparks and were often observed playing and talking with other kids

Visits to the Interactive Galleries Vary

The MUV study found that between 10 percent and 22 percent of family visitors in all three museums made the interactive gallery their first stop. Family visitors to all three museums were equally likely to stop at the interactive galleries during the middle of their visit. Roughly 20 percent of family visitors at each museum visited the interactive gallery after or before visiting the collections or exhibitions galleries.[27]

The Frist Art Museum's Martin ArtQuest Gallery is located adjacent to exhibition spaces, making multiple stops easy. However, only a few families took this opportunity. The Speed Art Museum's ArtSparks family gallery is located on the basement level of the museum, so it is no surprise that few families stopped in more than once during a single visit.[28]

The High Museum of Art's Greene Family Learning Gallery is located fairly near the entrance to the museum in one of the multiple buildings on campus, and it is on the way to the area where family and children's programs are held. This made it easier for families to visit the Greene Family Learning Gallery before and after attending a program (figure 3.6).[29]

The Magellan family made their first visit to the High Museum of art in the summer of 2007; Amelia was age five, Christopher age two, and Alexander was just a few months old. After reading about the High Museum's Thursday and Saturday art studio activities, Isabella, the mother, decided to explore the activities with her children.

Figure 3.6. Young boy at drawing board in the Greene Family Learning Gallery at the High Museum of Art, Atlanta, Georgia. Used by permission: Marianna Adams, Photographer

On two occasions, the family visited the Greene Family Learning Gallery first, and on another, they visited the family space somewhere in the middle. On every occasion, the family took a "lunch break" during the middle of the visit and participated in an art-making event (Summer Break Studios and Toddler Thursday). During two visits, the family viewed a special exhibition (*First Emperor* and *Monet Water Lilies*).

Isabella described visits to the High Museum as "low maintenance . . . something for everyone," and a place where Amelia, Christopher, and Alexander could interact with other children and be creative. She also said that having a place to take the children to play and run around during the winter and summer when it was either too cold or hot to play outside was an important benefit. Spending most of their time in the Family Gallery was the most important aspect of their visits, "more important than the exhibit, says Isabella." When Marco, her husband, or other adults were present, the adults took turns watching the children in the Greene Family Learning Gallery, while the other adults went upstairs to view the galleries or special events. She noted that without the Greene Family Learning Gallery, her family would go to the art museum much less frequently and would not have a membership because the children were too young to last long in the galleries, which would make visiting not worth the cost of admission. As Isabella said: "It is something the whole family can do and enjoy together and it is different from playing at home and they get to see things they normally don't get to see and run around."

Visits to the Interactive Gallery are Last

One of the hypotheses that inspired our FLING study concerned the commonly accepted notion in the museum field that a family interactive gallery would help to launch families into the museum proper. However, both of our research studies found that families tended to use the interactive spaces as "carrots" or "kick-back" spaces after first visiting the museum collections and exhibitions.[30] Parents in the case studies often said that they kept children attentive in the galleries by promising them a visit to the interactive space at the end. Other parents noted that the interactive space was a place where parents and children could relax as behavioral expectations (as in no touching, loud talking, or playfulness) in the interactive spaces were relaxed. In slightly more than one-third of the observed visits to the three art museums (seventeen out of forty-nine visits), the interactive space came last in the order of the visit, supporting parent's observation that these types of spaces served as behavioral incentives for children.[31]

When asked why they visit the Greene Family Learning Gallery at the High Museum of Art last on one of their accompanied visits, a mother explained "we always go in the end because she has been listening to 'don't run, don't run' and so we come here at the end and she knows that and she gets to play for a while and that is what she does, she sits and builds and climbs all over."[32]

Joy and Kelly Carlisle made their first visit to the Frist the weekend it opened in 2001. Joy, the mother, recalled that she and her daughter Kelly (around one year old at the time) sat and made little fashion and paper dolls together. A native Nashvillian, Joy noted that she first visited the Frist because it was "big news" and that she was sure it would be a "positive influence in the community." Joy also recalled that after their first visit to the museum that day, she "knew that the Frist would be part of Kelly's life, but didn't realize it would be AS big a part of her life as it has been."

In talking about their motivation for visiting the Frist Art Museum and Martin ArtQuest, Kelly and Joy emphasized the hands-on nature of the learning and how that type of learning created an "opportunity to hook [children] on the next level of learning." Joy also referred to Martin ArtQuest as a "bargaining chip or carrot" that gets children into the galleries. During their first observed visit to the Frist for this project, Chris, the father, and Joy explained that Martin Art-Quest "is a great place for recreation and learning" and that "sometimes she gains both and sometimes just one element." Chris also added: "that does not bother me; I don't want to push her."

During their three accompanied visits to the Frist Art Museum, the Carlisle Family followed the same visit pattern: exhibitions first and Martin ArtQuest last. On the first visit, Chris joined Joy and Kelly. The second and third visits more closely resembled what Joy described as a typical visit with only Kelly and Joy on the visit. When the father was present on the first visit, the family only looked at the first artwork in the galleries together before splitting up and wandering off in their own directions, spending a few seconds at each artwork before moving on. Not much conversation took place between the family during this visit, although they smiled at each other and exuded an overall sense of well-being and comfort with what they were doing. When they did speak to each other while in the galleries, they almost always did so in whispers.

On other visits, when just Joy and Kelly were present, the two tended to stay closer together, although there were still times when they viewed artworks on their own. Both mother and daughter read labels, often doing so aloud so that the other person could hear. Joy and Kelly engaged in frequent dialogues and conversations about the artwork on both visits. Overall, the conversations were very back and forth, with each person asking and answering questions and moving the conversation forward. At all times, Joy displayed a great deal of nurturing toward Kelly, asking questions that would enable her to work independently. The bond between the mother and daughter always seemed close, natural, and organic.

While in Martin ArtQuest, Kelly tended to focus on anywhere from two to four stations during a visit. Sometimes she worked alone, while mother, and father on the one visit, observed Kelly. While creating artwork, the family tended to work quietly, with Kelly sometimes humming or talking quietly to herself. On a few occasions, Joy sat and read quietly while Kelly created her artwork.

CONNECTIONS AT HOME AND LONG AFTER

A visit to a museum does not occur as a solitary event that begins when the family enters through the revolving doors and ends when they return to their car. Various studies of families in museums suggest that parents often have postvisit discussions with their children in the car, back at home, or during other family events.[33] For example, families who frequently visit museums (including art museums) often discussed their visit over dinner or referred to it when engaged in a related activity later on.[34]

Another question we asked ourselves at the outset of the FLING research project was: How do families integrate their art museum experiences into their daily lives or how do those experiences support their learning agendas, family values, and family relationships?

The large-scale MUV study found that approximately 80 percent of families tended to strengthen these connections at home through family discussions, as well as through engaging in art-making activities inspired by their art museum and interactive gallery experience.[35]

The LCS followed seventeen families, across the three participating museums, over eighteen months. Each family was accompanied by a researcher on visits to the museum. This was an opportunity to engage in multiple conversations over an extended period of time so we better understood how the museum visit creates lasting memories within families. These parents went to great lengths to situate a family leisure learning experience within a larger context of the child's life. They looked for opportunities to connect the art and interactive gallery activities with personal interests and lessons learned at school.[36]

Just before publishing this book, we checked back in with a few families who participated in the FLING LCS in 2009–2010 to see what they remembered and how they thought the experience benefited the family. We were gratified that so many of the key benefits and values found in our FLING studies remained ten years later.

The Magellan[37] Family, High Museum of Art

The Magellan family has since relocated from Atlanta to California (figures 3.7 and 3.8). When asked her memories of how their repeated visits to the High Museum supported her as a mother of young children, she responded: "There was always enough to do that it could be a long visit. It was worth the drive. Sometimes the kids were bored in twenty minutes in other places. It definitely felt like there was something for all of them to do. It wasn't just geared for toddlers."

Figure 3.8.   The Magellan family in 2020. Used by permission: The Badgett Family

Figure 3.7.   The Magellan family in 2009. Used by permission: Marianna Adams, Photographer

The boys were quite young in 2010 so have no memories of the High Museum or of participating in the study, but the daughter, Amelia, was six and now, at age sixteen, has a few specific memories of things she saw (the Chinese Terracotta Warriors exhibition in spring–summer 2009) and did (painted on easels in the museum's studio space). Amelia says she is interested in studying art and history in college and wants to explore working in a museum. We asked when she realized her interest in museums. She said she's always liked art and history but just recently started thinking about museums as a career. She said: "I didn't realize that until this fall when I found out it was a career. But I looked back on my childhood and remembered I was most happy when at museums."

The Gnome Family, Speed Art Museum

The Gnome family still live near the Speed Art Museum. Mama Gnome echoed a similar memory to Isabella Magellan from the High Museum of Art: "It was nice to have a quality resource close by and there were enough different things to see and do at ArtSparks. It satisfied both kids with different interests and almost four years apart in age." When asked how the museum supported her family she said: "Part of our job as parents is helping the kids learn and know what's outside of themselves. It's fundamental. I can't imagine not doing it. [Going to museums.] It's part of being an educated person."

In 2009 at a meeting of all six families participating in the LCS at the Speed Art Museum, they were asked to think of a family story that has become part of the family lore, told at holidays and family gatherings and create a visual representation expressing some aspect

Figure 3.9. Artifact to illustrate a family story that became mythic, created by the Gnome family at the Speed Art Museum, 2009. Used by permission: Marianna Adams, Photographer

of that story. We designed this activity to be a fun way to get to know each other. Mama Gnome had a specific memory of that experience and said they still have the artworks they made that night displayed in their home. Figure 3.9 shows a visual expression of a story passed down on Papa Gnome's side of the family

about an ancestor who was conscripted into the Czar's army in Russa.

The Cleaver Family, Speed Art Museum

The Cleaver family still live in the Louisville, Kentucky, area. The Cleavers' older daughter, Wallis (now age twenty) recalls ArtSparks as the place where "we got to get our energy out." Wallis also had a clear memory about her mother, June, going through the Museum's American Indian collection looking for inspiration for a costume for her elementary school class project. "She asked my opinion a lot. She was looking at head dresses and the necklaces for the hand puppet."

The Cleavers are a family of avid museum-goers. When asked why, June replied: "probably it's my influence [the whole family agreed here]. My mother was a docent at Speed for over twenty years. That rubbed off on me and I'm trying to rub off on my kids. I think creativity is the most important thing. The museum gives me different ways to think about things, different perspectives."

Both Cleaver daughters, Wallis and Theodora (now age seventeen), were articulate about how they think they benefited from going to the Speed and to all the museums they've visited with their family.

Wallis: "It inspired me to appreciate art more. It led to me to want to make my own art. I enjoy painting. I enjoy reading books and I look at art, so I make a connection between the two. With the influence of my mom, I've been able to enjoy all types of art."

Figure 3.10. The Cleaver family in 2009. Used by permission: Marianna Adams, Photographer

Figure 3.11. Fernando Botero, *Family Scene 2*, 1969, oil on canvas. Used by permission: Berardo Museum, Collection of Modern and Contemporary Art, Lisbon, Portugal

Figure 3.12. Cleaver family portrait 2020, inspired by Botero's *Family Scene 2*. Used by permission: The Dunham Family

Theodora: "I'm a creative person in general. [Mom chimes in: "very creative."] I guess going to a museum enhances my ability to be creative more widely. I like to paint a lot—sometimes I paint abstract paintings I think of, or maybe go on Pinterest and use that to put my own interpretations on it."

When Theodora's school was shut down in April 2020 due to the coronavirus disease 2019 (COVID-19) pandemic, she had to finish up the year online. As part of a project for her humanities class, Theodora selected a painting by Ferdinand Botero and arranged her family to interpret and expand upon Botero's composition. See figure 3.10 of the Cleaver family in 2009 and figures 3.11 and 3.12 of Theodora's humanities project family portrait.

YOUR TURN
When you are designing your family interactive space, consider the following questions:

1. Where will the space be located, and how might that location affect where in the larger museum visit families might go there?
   The FLING study found that where the interactive space was located in the museum had an effect on when families visited it.
2. How do you expect the family space will serve visitors?

The museum educators in the FLING study stated at the outset that their spaces were designed as launching pads, ways to entice families into the museum and then move them out into the galleries. This expectation did not align with the data. Consequently, these museum educators have realigned their expectations with the ways in which families actually use the spaces. Will your space be a relax and kick back experience? Will it require parents or caretakers to assist or work with children?

3. Given the findings from various research studies, what are the implications on how you need to market the space?
4. What will the role of museum staff or volunteers be in your interactive space?
   Families indicated the importance of staff and volunteers in the spaces to facilitate their experience. How will this knowledge result in staffing decisions at your museum? How will it influence training of staff and volunteers?

So when we *stop*, *look*, and *listen* to what families are really doing, it can inform our practice in transformative ways. Parents and caregivers are not bringing their children to the museum first to learn about art, but in fact, their primary goals are to learn about themselves, to learn about each other, and to be good parents, who are providing developmentally appropriate experiences for their children.

NOTES

1. Diamond, 1986; Sterry, 2004; Kelly, Savage, Griffin, and Tonkin, 2004; Luke, Ong, and Figueiredo, 2011(b); Yoshimura, Krebs, and Ratti, 2016.
2. Dierking, 1989; Ellenbogen, 2003.
3. Diamond, 1986.
4. Diamond, 1986.
5. Adams and Ancelet, 2011.
6. Ellenbogen, 2002
7. Kelly, et al., 2004, 41
8. Ellenbogen, 2003; Luke, et al., 2011(b).
9. Adams and Ancelet, 2011.
10. Luke, et al., 2011(b).
11. Ibid.
12. Ibid.
13. Adams, 1999.
14. This question was not a formal part of any of our surveys. It is our opinion based on multiple informal conversations with dozens of museum educators over fifteen years.
15. Adams and Ancelet, 2011.
16. Ibid.
17. Ibid.
18. Ibid.
19. The Learning Behaviors were adapted from Bloom's Cognitive and Affective Taxonomy as discussed in Anderson, Krathwohl, and Bloom, 2001; Simpson, 1972; Dave, 1970.
20. Adams and Ancelet, 2011.
21. Ibid.
22. Ibid.
23. Luke, et al., 2011(b)
24. Ibid.
25. Adams and Ancelet, 2011.
26. Families in the FLING LCS each got to choose their own "code names" for both their family name and their individual given names.
27. Luke, et al., 2011(b)
28. Adams and Ancelet, 2011; Luke, et al., 2011(b).
29. Ibid.
30. Adams and Ancelet, 2011; Luke, et al., 2011(b).
31. Adams and Ancelet, 2011.
32. Adams and Ancelet, 2011
33. Kelly, et al., 2004; Stein and Luke, 2006.
34. Ellenbogen, 2002.
35. Luke, Ong, and Figueiredo, 2011(c).
36. Adams and Ancelet, 2011.
37. All of the case study families selected their own aliases. No real names are used.

REFERENCES

Adams, M. *Summative Evaluation Report of the Art Learning Center Art Sparks Interactive Gallery at the Speed Art Museum, Louisville, KY* (unpublished evaluation report). Annapolis, MD: Institute for Learning Innovation, 1999.

Adams, M., and J. Ancelet. *Longitudinal Case Study Summaries.* 2011. Accessed October 28, 2020, at www.artmuseumfamilyspaces.org.

Anderson, L. W., D. R. Krathwohl, and B. S. Bloom. *A Taxonomy for Learning, Teaching, and Assessing: A Revision of Bloom's Taxonomy of Educational Objectives,* Complete ed. New York: Longman, 2001.

Dave, R. H. "Psychomotor Levels." In R. J. Armstrong, ed., *Developing and Writing Behavioral Objectives,* 20–21. Tucson: Educational Innovators Press, 1970.

Diamond, J. "The Behavior of Family Groups in Science Museums." *Curator,* no. 29(2) (1986): 139–54.

Dierking, L. "The Family Museum Experience: Implications from Research." *Journal of Museum Education,* no. 14(2) (1989): 9–11.

Ellenbogen, K. *From Dioramas to the Dinner Table: An Ethnographic Case Study of the Role of Science Museums in Family Life.* (Dissertations Abstracts International, 64(03), 846A. University Microfilms No. AAT30-85758) 2003.

Falk, J. H., and L. D. Dierking. *The Museum Experience Revisited.* Walnut Creek, CA: Left Coast, 2013.

Kelly, L., G. Savage, J. Griffin, and S. Tonkin. *Knowledge Quest: Australian Families Visit Museums.* Sydney: Australian Museum & the National Museum of Australia, 2004.

Luke, J. J., A. Ong, and C. Figueiredo. *Research Brief #1: Who Uses Dedicated, Interactive Galleries in Art Museums, and Why Do They Use Them?* Technical research report. Edgewater, MD: Institute for Learning Innovation, 2011(a). www.artmuseumfamilyspaces.org.

———. *Research Brief #2: How Do Families Use Dedicated, Interactive Galleries in Art Museums?* Technical research report. Edgewater, MD: Institute for Learning Innovation, 2011(b). www.artmuseumfamilyspaces.org.

———. *Research Brief #3: What Do Parents Value about Dedicated Interactive Galleries in Art Museums?* Technical research report. Edgewater, MD: Institute for Learning Innovation, 2011(c). www.artmuseumfamilyspaces.org.

Simpson, E. J. *The Classification of Educational Objectives in the Psychomotor Domain.* Washington, DC: Gryphon House, 1972.

Stein, J., and J. Luke. *Family Learning Project: Year 2 Evaluation* (unpublished evaluation report). Annapolis, MD: Institute for Learning Innovation, 2006.

Sterry, P. "An Insight into the Dynamics of Family Group Visitors to Cultural Tourism Destinations: Initiating the Research Agenda." Paper presented at the New Zealand Tourism and Hospitality Research Conference, Wellington, New Zealand, 2004.

Yoshimura, Y., A. Krebs, and C. Ratti. "An Analysis of Visitors' Length of Stay Through Noninvasive Bluetooth Monitoring in the Louvre Museum." *Computer Science, Physics.* 2016. https://arxiv.org/pdf/1605.00108.pdf.

CHAPTER 4

Walk the Talk

IF YOU CAN'T PRACTICE WHAT YOU PREACH, IT'S TIME to get out of the pulpit! So, now we're ready to walk the talk. Good design thrives on a strong understanding of the value of reflective practice and that practice is steeped in careful consideration of research findings. In this chapter we share our best practices based on years of research and observations focused on the motivation, use, and value that families find in interactive museum spaces. The museum educators at each art museum participating in the FLING study (Anne Henderson and Samantha Andrews, the Frist Art Museum; Julia Forbes, High Museum of Art; and Cynthia Moreno, the Mint Museum, formerly of the Speed Art Museum) each present a case study of how research has informed and transformed their practice. From digging into the research, to the initial vision documents, and to the concept development, we present our individual approaches to reflective practice as a true key to our collective successes.

FRIST ART MUSEUM MARTIN ARTQUEST GALLERY: CASE STUDY

Samantha Andrews and Anne Henderson

Introduction

The Frist Art Museum (FAM) in Nashville, Tennessee, is home to the four-thousand-square-foot Martin ArtQuest (MAQ) Gallery. FAM opened in 2001 as a noncollecting institution with a vision to inspire people to see their world in new ways through art and a mission to offer high-quality exhibitions with related educational programs and community engagement activities. It was the culmination of almost a decade-long civic dialogue and planning process in the 1990s led by the Frist Foundation that brought the Frist Center for the Visual Arts into being. The institution relied on the community's input again when its name was changed to the Frist Art Museum in 2018. With an average of twelve to fifteen exhibitions per year, visitors have seen exhibitions from all the continents—except Antarctica—as well as from premier art institutions around the world. Artists of all eras

and styles have been presented at the Frist, including international and local artists, college and K–12 students, teaching art faculty, and community artists. These exhibitions also represent a diversity of artistic creativity and mediums: assemblages, cars, decorative arts, fashion, glass, installations, manuscripts, paintings, performances, photography, prints, sculpture, textiles, and videos.

MAQ, an integral component of the institution since its inception, has been a constant favorite of visitors of all ages. It is seen as a place to explore art, creativity, and imagination. The hands-on, accessible stations provide individuals and small groups opportunities to explore a range of art-making media—drawing, printmaking, animation, painting, and sculpture—each using high-quality materials with the support of professional educators. The educational approach to creating MAQ was based on enduring understandings of art, a strong focus on the elements and principles of art, and offering visitors opportunities to look at, talk about, and make art all in response to the changing exhibitions at FAM (figure 4.1).

MAQ's location, adjacent to the upper-level galleries, sets the space apart from interactive galleries in other art museums that are often located on lower levels or away from the main galleries. Here, everyone is invited into MAQ to explore, create, and make connections in response to what they have seen and experienced in the nearby adjacent galleries.

MAQ's footprint also extends well beyond the museum. The Frist Art Museum's education team creates companion programming that is available online, including lesson plans and evergreen minute-long art videos that teachers may draw on for their classrooms grouped into four categories: Connect, Create, Explore, and Discover. In collaboration with Nashville Public Television, FAM produced *ArtQuest: Art is All Around You*, which won 2013 and 2014 Emmy Awards from the Mid-South Chapter of the National Academy of Television Arts and Sciences for Children's Programming (figure 4.2). These resources and

Figure 4.1.   Frist Art Museum, Nashville, Tennessee. John Schweikert, photographer; Used by permission: Frist Art Museum

other related home and classroom activities are found online at FristKids.org.

The family audience is an integral part of the FAM's 2017–2021 Strategic Plan. Families were part of the four major (but not exclusive) segments of the community identified as a focus during this strategic plan: (1) families and children; (2) museum visitors seeking contemplative and meaningful experiences with art; (3) diverse audiences, especially nontraditional museum visitors and those with special needs; and (4) pedestrian traffic, tourists, and a youthful demographic. The MAQ renovation was a key strategic goal for 2018. In addition, staff was tasked with continuing to seek visitor input on the space, as well as having a regular peer review.

Also, in 2017, the FAM board of trustees made an intentional commitment to Diversity, Equity, Access, and Inclusion (DEAI) with the adoption of an official policy to reinforce the institutional commitment to mandates and core values established at the founding. Since then, staff and trustees have pursued the development of an implementation plan and are currently working to deepen the commitment through the creation of a detailed plan with strategies, measurable goals, and a timeline. Frist educators review programs and activities to ensure all the DEAI goals are part of the planning process.

FLING Study Key Takeaways

The FLING study allowed us to understand visitation patterns and see the full family experience—

ARTQUEST
Art is All Around You!

Figure 4.2.   ArtQuest: *Art is All Around You Logo.* Used by permission: Frist Art Museum

exhibition galleries and MAQ, and sometimes the café and gift shop—in a new light. On average, families in the MUV study split their time evenly between the exhibition galleries and MAQ, with the visit to MAQ following time spent with the exhibitions—the reverse of what staff anticipated.[1] Families stressed the importance and the value of interactive galleries in art museums to offer a place that stimulates interesting discussions, a place to understand and love art, and an enjoyable experience for the whole family.[2] In the LCS, we also saw commonalities between the museum experience and other family leisure activities. For example, the experiences met the varied interests of family members while reinforcing family values; the experiences were active—not passive; there were opportunities for family conversation; and the spaces sparked creativity, imagination, independent thinking, and self-expression.[3]

Conversations with case study families revealed the significant value they placed on interactive galleries. They are seen as safe places to relax and unwind while engaging in rich sensory activities that foster a love and understanding of art. The interactive gallery provided freedom for children—the ability to explore and engage in creative play, together or independently. Older, self-directed children tended to choose their own activity. As one teenager explained, the interactive gallery helped them realize "that I am a creative soul." Unsurprisingly, the most frequent learning behavior observed was looking at art, followed by explaining, identifying, and evaluating. Smaller trends in learning behaviors were reading, self-reflection, interpreting, describing, inviting, remembering, and confirming.[4]

Understanding the behavioral patterns of families influenced our approach to the complete renovation of the space in 2018 and to ensuring that the new MAQ was both an integrated, as well as a stand-alone experience for families.

Learning in the Twenty-First Century

At the inception of MAQ, current art educational theory and practice focused on talking about and making art, as well as making meaningful connections. As educational theory evolved, so did museum interactive spaces. Policy makers and education leaders sought new pathways to prepare learners for success in our rapidly changing, information-driven world. The movement to embrace twenty-first-century learning skills became a universal, human response to society's rush toward a tech-integrated social and economic environment and the need to equip learners with flexibility and innovation. With the fostering of primary and critical skills—Creativity, Critical Thinking, Communication, and Collaboration (the 4 C's)—education was retooled to amplify not only the knowledge but also the individual learner's skills necessary for a changing world. As one's confidence and adaptability are increased, this fosters empowerment and ownership over an individual's experiences. The concept of "edutainment" manifested in new and exciting ways within informal learning spaces across the United States. Educational experiences were elevated through new venues of exploration like gamification, and physical, tactile experiences were enhanced with opportunities geared toward process rather than product. Additionally, experiential, hands-on learning was garnering new interest from teens and adults in our increasingly screen-dominated world.

FLING's MUV study told us that our visitors desired to learn not only art-making skills but also social skills.[5] Families became accustomed to museum experiences designed to engage the whole family in enjoyable, meaningful ways. FAM educators began developing new concepts in learning with multiple entry points and multifaceted outcomes. Nearly twenty years after the concept of twenty-first-century learning was introduced, it is still valid and evolving, spreading across the world with some seeing a fifth C, "Contributing," becoming part of the natural progression of the movement.

As MAQ's new design was developed, the FAM's education team used progressive learning models incorporating the twenty-first-century framework while continuing to nurture artistic interests and skills across generations and using lessons learned from FLING. The design responds to both the prevalent cultural interest in hands-on learning, and an upsurge in the popularity of shared learning experiences. MAQ's friendly art educators and volunteers continue to welcome and encourage visitors and guide their exploration of both looking at and creating art, through quality interactions that visitors can enjoy repeatedly, with different results each time. MAQ participants will continue to "grow up" in the space as they develop their artistic voices and interpret FAM exhibitions.

Accepting Change

During the research phase of the 2018 MAQ renovation, we quickly recognized we should not "throw the baby out with the bath water." MAQ in theory and value was "not broken," but we needed to identify the space's strengths and weaknesses, keep components that were successful and beloved, and approach change cautiously, with an eye to the future. We learned through FLING that families use museums to learn about themselves, the world, and one another.[6]

Our forever goal of "meeting the learner where they are" imbued meaning and intent as MAQ's overall space, individual ArtStations, and activities were reimagined with the contemporary learner in mind. Tiered learning goals that begin with the 4 C's distill temporary exhibition content into unique low-tech, high-tech, individual, and group experiences. And as it was from the beginning, MAQ facilitators and volunteers continue to ensure positive, visitor-focused encounters with the educational content. Some highlights from the MAQ renovation plan included:

- a bright, open entrance where visitors are greeted;
- full glass doors (replacing solid black ones) that connect MAQ to other education spaces, inviting visitors to move freely between galleries and studios;
- flexible space near the front of the gallery to create and showcase sizable collaborative art projects and community sculptures;
- an LED-lit wall where participants can explore light and color as they create large-scale patterns and designs;

- enlargement of the popular baby and toddler area to allow more participation through both tactile exploration and a reading nook;
- reconfiguration of the large art-making stations to improve functionality, encourage collaboration, and offer access to high-quality materials;
- expansion of the animation station to accommodate more participants and provide room for collaboration and creativity;
- an innovative transmedia station where visitors' movements interact with technology and with each other to create imaginative shapes and forms; and
- accessibility to all ArtStations, activities, and areas of the space for visitors of all abilities.

Elevating the Aesthetic

The MAQ gallery's 2018 renovation project occurred simultaneously with the FAM's larger rebranding initiative, transitioning from the Frist Center for the Visual Arts to the Frist Art Museum. A minimalist aesthetic was universally embraced to simplify communications in print, online, and in environmental design. FAM's new look was a welcome refresh that felt modern but complemented the museum's 1933 art-deco building.

When choosing a design firm, we looked for a team who presented fresh, new ideas about incorporating FAM's modernized aesthetic (figure 4.3). Our

Figure 4.3. Martin ArtQuest Rendering by Roto Design Group for 2018 renovation. Used by permission: Roto Design Group & Frist Art Museum

concerns were valid—would this approach to design create a *less* welcoming environment? Would a drastic change to the appearance of our space somehow affect its meaning? Would continuing our historic building's visual story into the MAQ space somehow fall flat with our multigenerational audience? In the end, once the space was realized, visitors of all ages embraced the new design and space.

Overall Design: Minimalism, Safety, Durability, and Flexibility

With a nod to our art-deco roots, the new design successfully married functionality and beauty. In the FLING study, parents regarded both physical and psychological safety as a value of the interactive gallery. A societal trend toward minimalist design in the twenty-teens ushered in associations between clean lines and open space with physical cleanliness and safety. Creating a comfortable space for our visitors meant clear sight lines, bright light, and easy-to-clean surfaces. A minimalist color palette not only provides a backdrop for the people, artwork, and activities in MAQ to be in full focus, but research also told us that it aids in early developmental learning and accessibility. MAQ not only serves individuals and families but also large groups, so durable surfaces are key to the space's longevity. FAM's ever-changing exhibition cycle requires great flexibility in the design of the individual ArtStations. The renovation provided an opportunity to create tiered interpretive experiences in new and exciting ways: Educators could update graphics, didactics, activities, and manipulatives in varying degrees quickly and easily thanks to the innovative and highly flexible ArtStation design.

While MAQ's physical footprint stayed the same, the renovation greatly opened up the existing space, expanded its functionality and flexibility, and created clear sight lines (figure 4.4). Accessibility for all visitors remained a core commitment in the renovation. To address environmental issues that affect visitors, sound baffling was added to reduce noise, and light and contrast were increased to improve visibility throughout the gallery. New technology elements were added to enhance visitors' participation in activities on multiple levels and encourage them to share their creations with their social media circles.

Equity and Access

Education is at the core of the FAM's mission with a priority on arts access to those eighteen years old and younger. Free admission for this group not only re-

Figure 4.4. Martin ArtQuest Gallery Entrance 2018. John Schweikert, photographer; Used by permission: Frist Art Museum

moves barriers for school, homeschool, and summer camp visitors, but also relieves the cost burden for the everyday family museum visitor. Access to MAQ is no different, with all types of learners using the space on a given day. Special attention was paid to MAQ's varied use in the redesign and a new space was dedicated to greeting visitors and distributing information (figure 4.5). Since the opening of the Frist, an ongoing relationship with the Tennessee Disabilities Coalition (TDC) allowed us to understand the needs of our visitors with varying abilities. As we approached the final stages of developing the new MAQ, consultants from the TDC advised us on how our updates may be adapted for equitable use. This resulted in the addition of a wheelchair-accessible sink, adjustments to the ArtStation design, and a comprehensive look at the presentation of informational didactics and manipulatives.

Representation Matters

The three-museum study from FLING told us that another factor in creating "a safe place" for visitors was fostering a sense of belonging.[7] Diversity and inclusion efforts have transformed FAM over the past ten years, changing the way we approach exhibition selection, programming, and staffing. In the new MAQ, it was critical for us to extend these efforts to the way we present information to our learners. Reevaluating our presentation methods made us recognize inclusivity was not complex. In reality, it could be found through simplification and equitable entry points. There is empowerment in self-sufficiency. MAQ didactics were redesigned with images accompanying text to accommodate the not-yet-reader and

Figure 4.5. Guests at Martin ArtQuest Gallery Animation Station. Tommy Lawson, photographer, Used by permission: Frist Art Museum

the non-English reader (figures 4.6 and 4.7). Images in didactics and designs for manipulatives were created to celebrate the diversity of MAQ's visitors, so they may encounter people who look like themselves when exploring MAQ's activities.

What's Next?

In 2019, the answer to "What's next for MAQ?" led to conversations about extending our efforts toward visitors with different abilities. The placement of an occupational therapy student intern in 2019 gave us greater insight on how we could better accommodate learners with dexterity challenges, or limited vision, hearing, or mobility. We began developing social stories and creating test spaces for visitors on the autism spectrum. Educators are excited about implementing this new and exciting research as we look ahead.

Future renovations and changes to the space will respond to changes in our world and social interactions. Families will continue to be the focus of this development, as will the need for visitors of all ages to experience the same creativity, wonder, and excitement in exploring the arts communally and individually.

About the Authors

Samantha Andrews, Assistant Director for Experiential Learning, Frist Art Museum, has served the Frist Art Museum in a variety of roles including visitor engagement, volunteer management, and experiential learning. For twenty years she has engaged people of varying ages and abilities, designed museum interactives, developed programs, and created experiential learning opportunities. Andrews has collaborated on two renovations to the Frist Art Museum's interactive space the Martin ArtQuest Gallery. She was the recipient of two Emmy awards for her work on the television series *ArtQuest: Art is All Around You* and developed the related website FristKids.org. Andrews has presented at various conferences including Southeastern Museums Conference, American Alliance of Museums, and National Art Education Association and was the Regional Director for the Southeast for the American Association of Museum Volunteers, 2009–2012.

Anne Henderson, Director of Education and Engagement at the Frist Art Museum, has more than thirty years of museum education experience

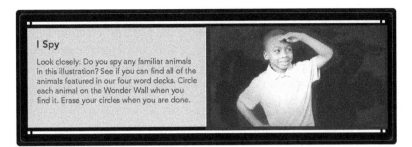

I Spy

Look closely: Do you spy any familiar animals in this illustration? See if you can find all of the animals featured in our four word decks. Circle each animal on the Wonder Wall when you find it. Erase your circles when you are done.

Figure 4.6. Example of Martin ArtQuest Gallery activity didactic. Used by permission: Frist Art Museum

at large and small institutions. She is the founding director of education and engagement at the Frist Art Museum, Nashville, and was previously at the National Gallery of Art, Washington, DC, and the Meadows Museum, Southern Methodist University, Dallas. She has served on various grant review panels for the Institute of Museum and Library Services (IMLS) and National Endowment for the Arts. She was the project director for an IMLS research grant on family learning in interactive galleries received

by the Frist Art Museum in partnership with the Speed Museum, Louisville, and the High Museum of Art, Atlanta. She currently oversees the education and engagement budget that includes visitor services and programming for adults, youth, families, community partners, and educators through workshops, lectures, multimedia programs, film series, tours, exhibition materials, outreach programs, and the interactive education gallery Martin ArtQuest Gallery.

Figure 4.7. Example of Martin ArtQuest Gallery Shadow Play animation scene. Used by permission: Frist Art Museum

HIGH MUSEUM OF ART GREENE FAMILY LEARNING GALLERY: CASE STUDY

Julia Forbes

A dedicated interactive space for families to learn, play, and explore has been part of the High Museum of Art since 1968. Since that time there have been ten different family gallery installations. During the FLING 2007–2011 study, the ninth family gallery (2005–2018) was the focus of our research (figure 4.8). This space was dedicated to a free-form style of creative play for toddlers through about age ten. An open space plan, the gallery comprised five hands-on activity areas: Building Buildings, Transforming Treasure, Making a Mark, Sculpting Spaces, and Telling Stories. These discovery activity areas were inspired by some of the most popular objects in the museum's collection.

The 2018 family gallery installation was part of the High's huge collections reinstallation and the new galleries, and the Greene Family Learning Gallery opened to the public together in October 2018. When we began planning for the tenth installation of the Family Learning Gallery in 2016, our first step was to review the FLING research findings. We identified the big takeaways from the study and incorporated them into the new space, which opened in October 2018. So committed to the family audience was our director, Rand Suffolk, that our square footage was doubled, from approximately two thousand square feet to slightly more than four thousand square feet, taking over space previously used for offices and a conference room.

We took this opportunity not only to celebrate the museum's fifty-year commitment to family audiences but, more importantly, to reenvision our relationship

with Atlanta's families. Our goal is to make the High Museum of Art an essential place for our community, where children and adults can engage together in informal learning, intergenerational communication, and play. These are fine words. Here is how we walked that talk.

Who Is Visiting?

Although we expected to see that the majority of our family visitors were mothers and kids, we were surprised to learn that most of these women considered themselves art enthusiasts. More than 70 percent identified themselves as people who create art for enjoyment and over 50 percent had taken art classes in the past. They tend to be regular visitors to our museum and 40 percent were members at the High. These mothers were also frequent visitors at other museums in the Atlanta area.[8]

Why Are They Visiting?

Internal evaluation we have conducted over the years confirms that most visitors come to the High Museum to see a special exhibition or participate in a program. This means that, for most families, the Greene Family Learning Gallery is not the primary reason for visiting the High Museum of Art because only 2 percent of visitors said their primary motivation for visiting was the family gallery.[9] It does, however, play a supporting role in a family's successful visit to the museum. Our family programs are an important motivation for about one-fifth of our family visitors and more than half of the visitors in our study participated in a family program. Parents also commented on the success of our family audio tours and reported reading labels together as a family.

Informing the Next Greene Family Learning Gallery Design

The FLING research that most informed our thinking for the 2018 (tenth) installation centered on when families use the learning gallery during their museum visit[10] and what they found most valuable about the space.[11]

First, we were surprised to learn that almost half of the visitors to the ninth Greene Family Learning Gallery did so at the end of their visit.[12] When we designed that space in 2005, we envisioned it as a starting point for families. Our reasoning was that if families had a place where they felt comfortable, we could use that time to orient them to the museum as a whole and help them plan a more effective visit to

Figure 4.8.   Greene Family Learning Gallery, High Museum of Art, 2005. Used by permission, Julia Forbes, photographer

Figure 4.9.   Family watches as child draws in the Greene Family Learning Gallery, 2006. Used by permission, High Museum staff photographer

Figure 4.10.   Family plays together at Greene Family Learning Gallery, 2018, ©CatMax, High Museum of Art. Used by permission, CatMax Photography

the galleries and exhibitions. We planned to provide a place to sign up for guided tours and offer self-guiding brochures and discovery backpacks to use in the larger museum. On paper, this seemed like a great idea. However, the FLING research told us that parents tend to use the Family Learning Gallery as an incentive for the children to behave while in the art galleries and a place to have some fun and blow off steam before they head home. They also tended to use the space as a type of holding activity while they waited for their special program to begin. Consequently, our efforts to prepare families to visit the larger museum went unused. It meant that in planning for our current (tenth) iteration of the Greene Family Learning Gallery we had to (1) rethink where we need to position the family tools designed to support gallery visits (e.g., self-guide brochures and tour sign-ups) and (2) design the Family Gallery activities to build on the experiences visitors have already had or not be dependent upon them at all.

Second, the study revealed that parents greatly valued the opportunity to spend quality time together.[13] For family audiences the social connection is most important. They see our institution as an enjoyable family leisure destination where memories are made. We realized that our ninth version of the Greene Family Learning Gallery did not provide enough opportunities for adults and children to participate together. This installation was primarily child focused with an emphasis on creative play, where the parent was more of an observer than an equal participant, as you can see in figure 4.9 where the parent is watching the child as she draws.

In the next installation we developed activities to encourage more meaningful interaction between the adults and children. As we worked with our designers on the tenth iteration of the gallery, we were mindful of this goal and came up with several activities that really engage adults and children in play together (see figure 4.10). For example, parents and children love working together, or sometimes side by side (grownups like to make art too) at the Community Tree to make works of art directly related to the High's collection and hanging them on the tree together.

Marketing Efforts to Families

When we learned that too many family visitors and, particularly, first-time visitors were not even aware that the Family Learning Gallery existed, we saw how a clearer marketing strategy could help us build a stronger and larger family audience (figure 4.11). In addition, we realized the importance of good customer service training for our front-of-house staff. If everyone who comes in contact with our visitors is aware of the programs and special experiences available, then they can appropriately direct families as they encounter them in the museum.

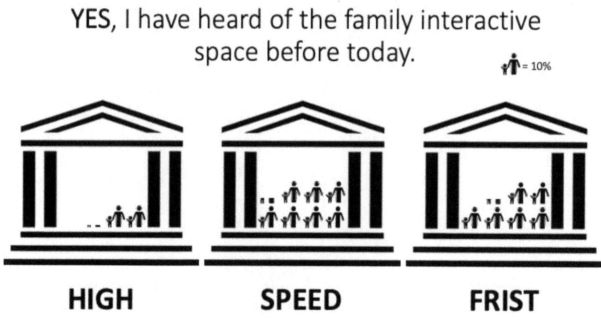

Figure 4.11. Fewer visitors at the High Museum of Art have heard of the family gallery than at the Speed and the Frist. Used by permission, Jessica Luke, et. al. (data) and Marianna Adams (graphic design)

Testing Our Ideas

We spent the summer of 2016 conducting a study to experiment and test activities for the new (tenth) 2018 Greene Family Learning Gallery. It was also an opportunity to listen to family visitors about what they would like to experience in such a space.[14] The findings of this study supported both studies in the FLING research results and provided specific insight into what types of experiences resonate most with families at the High Museum.

We took over a high visibility space in the museum, named it *Art Lab,* and invited our family visitors to test new activities and tell us what they wanted in a new space (figures 4.12, 4.13, and 4.14). We initiated a playful visitor response area, inviting people to respond to three different prompts.

1. If I could design a new family learning gallery it would definitely have . . .
2. I bring my family to the High Museum of Art because . . .
3. The greatest challenge I face when talking about art with my family is . . .

In addition, we conducted interviews and surveys with families who tested our activities.

What did we learn? We were excited to find that 84 percent of parents felt these new activities were designed for both adults and children. Clearly, we were strengthening the family bond. When asked about why their family visits the High Museum of Art, the four most frequently mentioned reasons were:

1. To increase our appreciation of art
   "My parents don't think I'm getting any culture watching Peppa Pig."
2. To look at art
   "We love seeing fun, funky, amazing, and great exhibits."
3. To have fun and enjoy ourselves
   "This is fun for the whole family."
4. To learn more about art
   "Understanding of art helps us understand the history of being human."

When asked to rate how much a list of statements reflected their experience in the Art Lab the visitors rated the following statements quite high:

- I had fun.
- I am more likely to perceive the High Museum of Art as a place that welcomes and values families.

Figure 4.12.   High Museum of Art, Art Lab, 2016. Used by permission, Julia Forbes, photographer

Figure 4.13.   Hearing from our visitors, High Museum of Art, Art Lab, 2016. Used by permission, Julia Forbes, photographer

Most Important Needs in a New Family Gallery

For Children	For Parents	For Family
1. Interact with Art 2. Stimulate their creativity and Imagination	1. Have a place to sit and observe while their children play 2. Learn new strategies to talk about art 3. Play with their children	1. Create a shared memory 2. Have fun together 3. Interact with art together 4. Use creativity and imagination 5. Make art together
• Parents perceive that young children learn best by interacting, exploring, and engaging the senses. • Parents perceived the art museum as being a unique environment where creativity and imagination are more likely to be sparked	What do parents perceive as their greatest challenge when discussing art with their families? • Not understanding or knowing how to explain art • Stimulating interest Parents seemed to have varying degrees of understanding of the nature and purpose of play, both for children and adults. Most adults appreciated play and saw it as something they wanted for their children.	Many parents emphasized the importance of creating shared memories, saying it is probably the main reason why they bring their families to the Museum Parents like to have fun and do things together and this includes both cooperative activities where adults and children work on the same thing, as well as "parallel play" where adults and children are both engaged in an activity while near each other.

Figure 4.14.   What do families want in a new Greene Family Learning Gallery? Results of 2016 front-end evaluation, Used by permission, High Museum of Art and Jeanine Ancelet

- I am more likely to perceive the High Museum of Art as a place to bring my family more than once.
- I stimulated my curiosity and wonder.
- I stimulated my creativity and imagination.
- I feel more confident facilitating art experiences for my child.

We took heart that we were on the right track, addressing some weaknesses revealed in the FLING 2011 study and more closely aligning the family experience with our vision for the new space.

Working with Our Community

In 2017, the museum brought together specialists in different aspects of education, early learning, design-thinking, accessibility, and special needs from the Atlanta community for a brainstorm around the new space (tenth version, 2018). From a graphic designer to a public-school kindergarten teacher, to a Reggio Emilia expert, to a STEM education leader and leader in working with children with disabilities, this group worked closely with us for more than a year, helping us to form our vision and intention statement (see Appendix A), develop our goals, and review and comment on the design plans as the process unfolded. These community members were also invaluable partners in testing our design concepts. A powerful moment occurred when we shared the plans for a climbing area that was adjacent to an area about texture. The kindergarten teacher offered, how about punching some holes in the wall between the two spaces, so the kids can see each other. That way the children who can't or don't want to climb can engage with each other. A terrific idea which we quickly employed. We invited them to their own special pre-press event walk-through to personally thank them for all their efforts. They are also each recognized on the High Museum's website.

Development Process

Our work with the community resulted in a clear "vision and intention document" that articulated what we want our family visitors to walk away with (how families benefit from the Family Learning Gallery experience), our conceptual/pedagogical framework (such as Reggio Emilia and the importance of a shared social experience), specific design issues (opportunities and constraints), and what we called "content puddles" as we did not want to define the exact content too soon. This document accompanied our request for proposals (RFPs) to approximately eight design firms.

The vision and intention document turned out to be a wonderful tool as we met with potential designers

and they made proposals in response to our RFP. The fact that we had done this work in advance of bringing on the designer and had offered the information to potential designer firms to inform their proposals, meant the proposals were stronger, the designers understood more clearly our goals and desired outcomes and when we finally settled on the winning firm, we really hit the ground running on our collaborative work process.

Marking the fiftieth anniversary of our commitment to family spaces, the High debuted a total redesign and expansion of the Greene Family Learning Gallery with new interactive environments in October 2018 (tenth version). We got even more attention for the new space as it was part of the museum's overall reinstallation project and, therefore, part of a huge press rollout. The new Greene Family Learning Gallery expanded to include a two-thousand-square-foot space across the hall from its previous footprint. The High's education department worked with Roto design firm to create the gallery's two distinct spaces based on a set of goals, which were informed by years of visitor observation, community expert input, and research. Each space offers a welcoming, safe, and fun environment that is child-centered and child-directed with age-appropriate activities for kids ranging from babies to eight-year-olds (figure 4.15). The open-ended, intuitive, multisensory elements, designed to be inclusive for all, combine cutting-edge technology with hands-on activities.

Our goals for the new Greene Family Learning Gallery were to:

- Offer a space for families to make memories while fostering stronger connections between caregivers and children.
- Empower children and their caregivers to explore the museum and more confidently engage with its collection.

Figure 4.15. Children playing in the Greene Family Learning Gallery, High Museum of Art, 2018, ©CatMax, High Museum of Art. Used by permission, CatMax Photography

Figure 4.16. Greene Family Learning Gallery, "Create," High Museum of Art, 2018, ©CatMax, High Museum of Art. Used by permission, CatMax Photography

Figure 4.17. Greene Family Learning Gallery, "Experience," High Museum of Art, 2018,©CatMax, High Museum of Art. Used by permission, CatMax Photography

- Inspire wonder and encourage children to be curious about the art they encounter every day.
- Celebrate creativity, imagination, empathy, and play, and help families develop these skills through one-of-a-kind interactive experiences found only at the High.

The original Greene Family Learning Gallery space became "CREATE," a bright and open studio devoted to developing young visitors' art-making abilities and centered on the creative process (figure 4.16). The newly created second Gallery space, "EXPERIENCE," is a deeply immersive gallery that enables visitors to explore what art means, how it feels, and where it can take us (figure 4.17). Each gallery space features a quiet space with activities designed for reflection and a chance to get away from the noisier, more active main rooms, as well as an area specifically for babies and toddlers.

THE MINT MUSEUM LEWIS FAMILY GALLERY AND SPEED ART MUSEUM ARTSPARKS: CASE STUDY

Cynthia Moreno

Shortly after our Speed, High, and Frist FLING project ended in 2011, I put on my traveling shoes and clicked my heels, ready for a new professional adventure. As I departed Louisville, the Speed Museum was about to close for a landmark expansion, and I joined the Mint Museum's Education Department in Charlotte, North Carolina, in large part, because of their commitment to family learning and the new Lewis Family Gallery. Consequently, this case study reflects on my experience at the Speed and ArtSparks and weaves the lessons learned there with our current practice at the Mint Museum.[15]

When I moved to Charlotte to work at the Mint, we began the first of many conversations on family learning. I could see the commonalities between the Speed and the Mint's approaches, which offered families of all ages a welcoming, creative place to grow together (figure 4.18).

During one of our first chats, I recall hearing my colleague, Leslie Strauss, reference an approach I used in Art Sparks to balance the activity temperature of areas. She noted that our idea of "cool, warm, and hot zones" was useful in thinking about how to distribute excitement levels on the floor plan. With my cross-country move, I felt like a time travel leap occurred. As I joined this new branch of museum practitioners, I saw myself in the mirror watching my colleagues apply learning and lessons from ArtSparks at the Speed Museum. I was struck by how Leslie and the Mint staff skillfully managed to navigate competing priorities and multiple shareholders to create an engaging space during a financial downturn. The Mint's new family gallery highlighted a variety of best practices including being centrally located on the main floor, using intuitive, photo-based didactics, and clear sightlines providing parents with peace of mind. Glass walls invited visitors to see the handsomely designed Lewis Family Gallery with generous wrap-around seating, which beckoned both children and adults (figure 4.19). Given our emphasis at the Speed on creating spaces for preschool children, it was affirming to see the Mint's featured space for crawlers and toddlers. The five activity zones showcase works from the museum's art and international design collection, including several works from the collection. Similar to the blend of multiaged activities used at the Speed, all ages are welcomed in the Lewis Family Gallery to create art, experiment with spatial building and puzzle challenges, engage in imaginative play, and collaborate on a community project.

After opening Art Sparks at the Speed Museum, we conducted our first evaluation study to create a shared language that described what we witnessed families doing and saying. A decade or so later, the FLING study collected and mapped a rich bank of family visitor data. Many of FLING's central findings about families, audiences, and motivations validated ideas we gleaned firsthand from watching families in the galleries. Mint staff also learned more about family behavior from informal gallery observations.

A key difference in the two museums was gallery staffing. Art Sparks at the Speed had dedicated paid and volunteer gallery staff available during open hours to provide assistance to families. As is the case with many art museum family spaces, the Mint originally planned to have gallery staff but shifted to self-guided experiences due to budget constraints. Akin to our approach at the Speed, the Mint's gallery was developed from a rich mosaic of sources; these pieces ranged from staff's own museum teaching ideas, surveying examples of interactivity in other museums, and listening to families' feedback on prototypes. When extended travel to experience family spaces in other museums wasn't a financial option, the Mint sought advice from a range of museum colleagues through phone interviews with peers, including reaching out to the Speed Museum and amassing a trove of articles, images, insights, and experiences. Staff also made

Figure 4.18.   Shadow Play activity at Art Sparks in the Speed Art Museum, Louisville, Kentucky. Janice Braverman, Photographer; Used by Permission: Speed Art Museum

visits to nearby family-friendly areas, ranging from IKEA, the High Museum, the GreenHill Center for North Carolina Art, science museums, playgrounds, and classrooms.

Figure 4.19.   Lewis Family Gallery in the Mint Museum, Charlotte, North Carolina. Jon Strayhorn, Photographer; Used by Permission: Mint Museum

Both the Speed and the Mint invested energy into the all-important prototyping process. Although both museums previously created interactive offerings within galleries and changing exhibitions, each institution was launching its first dedicated family gallery space. The Mint was fortunate to get an Institute of Museum and Library Services (IMLS) grant to develop and test gallery prototypes. ImaginOn, a unique Charlotte facility housing the children's library and theater, underwrote the project, turning it into an exhibition titled *Art Under Construction*. Area families were invited to help build the Mint's future family gallery by playing and giving feedback. Another thread of commonality between the two museums was that in addition to reaching our family-with-children audience, we wanted to remain welcoming to current museumgoers. Our definition of "family" is broader than the standard of adults with children. Family may include a group of senior citizens from a retirement community to college-age friends on an off-campus outing together, to an adult couple. With this recognition that "family" can mean many things, we design our experiences to make all ages feel welcomed and respected.

Supporting Creativity

We discovered that many parents are motivated to visit art museums to foster their children's creativity. Parents repeatedly told us that painting and making art should be part of a museum visit, so our gallery plans were adjusted to include a spacious hands-on art-making area.

Supporting families spending time together and making opportunities to play and learn from each other requires making our spaces equally friendly to both children and adults (figure 4.20). For example, in the Lewis Family Gallery's Imagination Station, the art-making space is adult-scaled so all ages can sit together to create. We often discover adults happily working away at a drawing in this large, open space while their children keep a watchful eye from the nearby playhouse.

The Power of Play and Inventive Use

> The house shelters daydreaming, the house protects the dreamer, the house allows the dreamer to dream in peace.
>
> —Gaston Bachelard, *Poetics of Space*[16]

Like Gaston Bachelard's metaphor of the house as a nest or shelter, museums can also serve as a powerful place for imaginative metaphoric thinking. Offering an artistic sanctuary, the museum is a safe haven to foster dreams, memories, and fantasies in ways that can have people returning again and again throughout their lifetime.

FLING parents shared with us their desire to have their children forge a lifelong connection with museums. The Speed's new mission statement "To celebrate art forever" captures the invitation to join the lifelong museum tribe in a compelling way. The Mint recently revised its mission statement to say, "The Mint welcomes all to be inspired and transformed through the power of art and creativity."

Figure 4.20. Exterior of Romare Bearden Playhouse at Lewis Family Gallery in the Mint Museum, Charlotte, North Carolina. Jon Strayhorn, Photographer; Used by Permission: Mint Museum

Figure 4.21. Mom offering cake at Lewis Family Gallery in the Mint Museum, Charlotte, North Carolina. Jon Strayhorn, Photographer; Used by Permission: Mint Museum

While many museum educators offer art-making activities, another creative activity is dramatic or imaginative play. Offering this powerful play option allows young children to connect emotionally with others while fostering empathy. Paired with or without art making, dramatic and imaginative play can help participants connect to stories, fellow humans, and the wider world (figure 4.21).

To connect children to the art of Romare Bearden, the Lewis Family Gallery planners initially wanted to let children explore the medium of collage. In prototype testing, children were first given large, magnetic shapes to layer inside a shotgun-style house, based on Bearden's collage, *Evening of the Gray Cat* (figure 4.22). However, something curious and magical happened. Children dismissed the magnetic activity and instead stepped into the house to own and rule over their play world. They busily created new families with other children who just moments ago had been total strangers, assigning chores and working together. All adults were suddenly seen as outsiders. Kids threw themselves into newfound work, cooking vegetables, hanging up the laundry, setting the table, and sweeping the floor. Based on the children's strong responses,

Figure 4.22. Romare H. Bearden (American, 1911–1988). *Evening of the Gray Cat,* **1982, collage on board. Gift of Bank of America. 2002.68.3. Collection of The Mint Museum, Charlotte, North Carolina. Used by Permission: © 2021 Romare Bearden Foundation / Licensed by VAGA at Artists Rights Society (ARS), New York**

the designers dropped the art instruction approach and instead added more imaginative play elements, like an interactive mural with moving parts.

In much the same vein, Art Sparks at the Speed Museum also offered immersive play environments. One popular area was inspired by works from the Speed's seventeenth-century Dutch Masters collection. The mock Dutch house had real delft tiles, a crackling faux fireplace, faux ham, bread, and pewter mugs and plates (figure 4.23). The faux Dutch ship was inspired by *A Frigate and Other Vessels on a Rough Sea*, a maritime painting by Ludolf Backhuysen in the Speed's collection (figure 4.24). The ship had a wooden gangplank, a pulley system to load cargo, and a stormy battle scene unfolding. We adults loved to watch children working together to pass pitchers of imaginary water from the Dutch house kitchen to extinguish an imaginary fire on the Dutch ship.

Seeing children become intensely creative, often in unexpected ways, is a beautiful phenomenon that I began to call "inventive use." The presence of inven-

Figure 4.24. Ludolf Backhuysen (Dutch 1630–1703), *A Frigate and Other Vessels on a Rough Sea*. Oil on canvas, Collection of the Speed Art Museum, Louisville, Kentucky 1995. Used by Permission: Speed Art Museum

tive use can signal to practitioners how fully children are engaging at the moment. Early on at the Speed, we started using the term "inventive use" to internally signal when children got immersed in their creative zone and started making highly original connections. Similar to stumbling upon a bird's nest in the forest, a child's creativity is both emergent and fragile. As educators we can often get prescriptive about how a creative play activity might go. By saying "Whoa! That's inventive use!" This reminds us to tread softly and let the creative genius of children have the space to play. Personal meaning and lasting memories are often made when children go off-script. Some examples of inventive use or imaginative play that we've observed include: fighting a fire, taking a custom meal to feed hungry parents outside of the house, or creating and pinning up themed artwork like "Home Sweet Home" or repainting a scene to customize the situation (figure 4.25).

Inspiring Reflective Practice

Observing life's moments and remaining a learner is a part of our museum educator DNA. Watching moments of discovery unfolding before us can inform experiences that we as museum educators seek to consciously create in our work. Through the active observation of situations that invite engagement, it is often easier to find the essence of an idea and engage the public. Trusting our intuition, observing, and gathering data has made us more courageous about what we do.

For me, a transforming aspect of the FLING project experience was having in-house evaluators on staff. At

Figure 4.23. Boy hoisting ropes on Dutch frigate at Art Sparks in the Speed Art Museum, Louisville, Kentucky. Used by Permission: Speed Art Museum

Figure 4.25.   Girl faux painting on pitcher at Lewis Family Gallery in the Mint Museum, Charlotte, North Carolina. Jon Stray-horn, Photographer; Used by Permission: Mint Museum

the Mint we've realized that "baking in" an internal evaluator role is an essential step toward becoming an active learning organization. Last year a colleague became our full-time Audience Research and Evaluation Specialist. It has been exciting to have a full-time partner to build evaluation into the core of our projects.

One of the most satisfying aspects of creating interactivity is that it can be like an encore performance. At the Mint, we've been asked to continue our efforts to make in-gallery special exhibition experiences fun and meaningful. We've learned how our participants use spaces and respond by conducting observations and interviews and using the data.

During the *William Ivey Long: Costume Designs* exhibition at the Mint, we gave visitors a long backlit drawing table and templates to draw and design costumes. Visitors (adults and children) who participated in the drawing activity told us that the hands-on activities really made them connect with the exhibition. Observing that our drawing area attracted 30 percent of visitors, we wondered what we could do to get a wider group of participants to engage in connecting activities. Would engaging in these activities increase participants' sense of meaning and connection?

We explored this question further while the Mint hosted an African textile exhibition from the Fowler Museum at UCLA. *African Print Fashion Now!* explored the symbols and tactile presence of the iconic African wax cloth. Since visitors couldn't touch the cloth in the exhibition, we gathered similar pieces of West and Central African wax cloth and Javanese batik to create our family gallery activity area (figure 4.26). The activities included a variety of multisensory modalities: arranging textile patches into different patterns, drawing your own fabric symbols, and a Symbol Hunt to find symbols within the exhibition's colorful fashions. The final activity was a Fabric Challenge (figure 4.27). We laughingly nicknamed this subtle activity "sleepy" because it looked like it would only attract serious textile types. The challenge started by reading a handful of aesthetic characteristics of two types of cloth: African wax cloth or Javanese batik. After reading clues, participants could look at, feel, and even smell the eight bolts of fabric and guess which bolts was which. Participants flipped a panel to discover how many matches they made.

In our visitor observations and interviews done during the two exhibitions, we saw some differences.

Figure 4.26.   Boy exploring *African Print Fashion Now!* Installation at the Mint Museum, Charlotte, North Carolina. Jon Stray-horn, Photographer; Used by Permission: Mint Museum

Figure 4.27. Family doing Fabric Challenge Activity at Mint Museum, Charlotte, North Carolina. Jon Strayhorn, Photographer; Used by Permission: Mint Museum

In contrast to the visitors who used the *William Ivey Long* drawing studio, twice the number of visitors participated in one or more activities in the *African Print Fashion Now!* exhibition. Gallery participants also told us that they most valued having tactile experiences and cited that as their main reason for participating. "I wanted to join in the whole museum experience. It's fun, hands-on, to create just after seeing the things in the exhibit." Numerous visitors let us know that while they liked all of the activities, many were taken with the subtlety of touching the fabrics and using their hands to assess the weight, texture, and patterns.

The presence of an interactive area within the museum can function as a living entity serving to humanize the museum. Over time these lively spaces with their returning participants may become like an internal heartbeat. Having families repeatedly visiting and growing up within our walls may reshape the museum in ways that largely have yet to be measured. However, seeing words like welcome, fun, and empathy along with phrases like "art for everyone" appearing in today's museum mission statements may reflect the impact of interactive gallery spaces.

About the Author

Cynthia Moreno is the Senior Director of Learning and Engagement at the Mint Museum in Charlotte, North Carolina. Moreno was previously Director of Education at the Speed Art Museum in Louisville, which is Kentucky's oldest and largest art museum, for eighteen years. There she directed innovative programs for schools, families, youth, and adults. She successfully implemented grant projects funded by major organizations including the National Endowment for the Arts and the Wallace Fund, and initiated numerous community partnerships. She founded the Speed's award-winning interactive gallery Art Sparks, which serves as a national model for engaging children and families in hands-on learning experiences. Working with colleagues at the High Museum of Art in Atlanta and Frist Art Museum in Nashville, she guided extensive research at the Speed on family learning in art museums. She has an active record of presentations and publications and has served in leadership roles with professional associations including the American Alliance of Museums, the National Art Education Association, and Southeastern Museum Association. Moreno has also been recognized by her peers as one of the outstanding art museum educators in the Southeastern United States. A Florida native, she received two B.A. degrees in Humanities and Mass Communications, and an M.A. in Art Education and Arts Administration from the University of South Florida.

NOTES

1. Luke, Ong, and Figueiredo, 2011(b).
2. Luke, Ong, and Figueiredo, 2011(c).
3. Adams and Ancelet, 2011.
4. Ibid.
5. Luke, et al., 2011(c).
6. Adams and Ancelet, 2011; Luke, et al., 2011(c).
7. Ibid.
8. Luke, Ong, and Figueiredo, 2011(a).
9. Luke, et al., 2011(a).
10. Adams and Ancelet, 2011; Luke, et al., 2011(b).
11. Adams and Ancelet, 2011; Luke, et al., 2011(c).
12. Luke, et al., 2011(c).
13. Adams and Ancelet, 2011; Luke, et al., 2011(c).
14. Ancelet, 2016.
15. Thanks to input from my valued colleague, Leslie Strauss, who oversees the Mint's family and studio programs and who developed the Mint's Lewis Family Gallery, which opened in 2010. Special appreciation goes to Gwendolyn Kelly, my longtime collaborator on Art Sparks and FLING evaluation assistant, for weaving in her insights.
16. Bachelard, 1964.

REFERENCES

Adams, M., and J. Ancelet. *Longitudinal Case Study Summaries*. 2011. Accessed October 28, 2020, at www.artmuseumfamilyspaces.org.

Ancelet, J. *Art Lab Evaluation Report for the High Museum of Art* (unpublished technical report). Davidsonville, MD: Audience Focus, 2016.

Bachelard, G. *The Poetics of Space*, translated by Maria Jolas. New York: Orion, 1964.

Luke, J. J., A. Ong, and C. Figueiredo. *Research Brief #1: Who Uses Dedicated, Interactive Galleries in Art Museums, and Why Do They Use Them?* Technical research report. Edgewater, MD: Institute for Learning Innovation, 2011(a). www.artmuseumfamilyspaces.org.

———. *Research Brief #2: How Do Families Use Dedicated, Interactive Galleries in Art Museums?* Technical research report. Edgewater, MD: Institute for Learning Innovation, 2011(b). www.artmuseumfamilyspaces.org.

———. *Research Brief #3: What Do Parents Value about Dedicated Interactive Galleries in Art Museums?* Technical research report. Edgewater, MD: Institute for Learning Innovation, 2011(c). www.artmuseumfamilyspaces.org.

CHAPTER 5

Get Started

READY TO CREATE AMAZING FAMILY SPACES?
NOW IT'S TIME TO GET TO WORK. THIS SECTION OF-
fers our best advice and lessons from our missteps
and successes. We'll share resources (with useful examples in the appendixes) such as checklists, guidelines, examples of visioning and intention statements,
examples of effective requests for proposals (RFPs),
practitioner-friendly ways to prototype and evaluate the success of interactive experiences, websites
or blogs for information and inspiration, and more.
We'll talk about budgets, marketing, and involving
your community in the process. A truly family-com-
mitted art museum finds that involving its community
in the design development process makes for a stronger project. We'll explore all of this through research,
best practices, stories, and reflections. Let's dive in!

How Do I Get Started?

The first key question is: Do you already have a
dedicated space for families or are you starting from
scratch? No matter what your answer is to that question, you'll want to start by building your team and
gathering support for your initiative. These are your
first steps toward envisioning what you want to create
and figuring out how to make it happen. There should
be two levels to your team: a larger museum, cross-
departmental team that includes educators, curators,
marketing staff, designers (even if you have an outside
design firm), and of course, museum leadership including your executive director and perhaps a trustee,
and a smaller core team who will attend weekly meetings and be the hard workers who get the project done.
You'll need a project manager, usually the person at
the museum responsible for the management of your
existing or your new family space, although some
museums find bringing in an experienced contractor
to manage the project supports their efforts better. It's
really about money, staffing, and time. Bottom line,
you want someone who intimately understands the
audience and space you want to create but also has

excellent attention to detail, is a terrific collaborator,
and knows how to manage a budget.

> Having clarity about roles and responsibili-
> ties; collaborative of course. I think the biggest
> challenge was communicating outcomes that
> incorporated ideas and functionality.
>
> —Anne Henderson, Director of Education
> and Engagement, Frist Art Museum,
> Nashville, Tennessee)

The timing of a big reinstallation or the adding of
a brand-new family space to your museum can make
all the difference in the world. Many art museum colleagues have found that pairing this huge undertaking
with a collections reinstallation or the addition of a
new building works extremely well. If you do this,
often the funding can be rolled into a larger fundraising effort, the museum will be bringing on contractors
that your project will need too (electricians, builders,
painters, etc.), so there is a cost savings, and the project becomes part of an overall public relations and
marketing push getting your hard work much more
attention and energy.

Another important step is figuring out what you
like. Do your research. Which museums and colleagues are doing interesting things in this arena? If
it's possible, you and a small team should visit as many
interactive spaces at a variety of types of museums as
you can. If travel is not possible, try setting up virtual
meetings with colleagues who have spaces that you'd
like to see. Make a chart to gather all your learnings
with headings like design, tech or no tech, look and
feel (super child focused or aimed at kids and adults),
square footage, open floor plan or several smaller
rooms, and so on. This is your chance to begin to hone
in on what would be most successful for your space
and your audience.

If you are starting from scratch and must advocate
for space, think like a real estate agent: location, loca-

tion, location. Our research has shown that interactive spaces that are easy to find and near high-traffic areas like entrances and exits get more attention and use. It can be hard to carve out space if the idea of interactive gallery was not part of the original architectural plan. Get creative, negotiate, advocate, and make sure your coalition within the museum is part of the effort.

Getting Your Feet Wet

If budgets are tight or your museum isn't ready to launch a big project, get your feet wet by trying something small and in-house. You can experiment by offering a custom, temporary space for three or six months dedicated to exploring a special exhibition or a collection gallery theme. A far-out, minimalist room or a quirky corner space in a gallery can surprise and engage visitors to make meaningful connections.

The silver lining of temporary interactive spaces is visibility and a great return on investment. Few live museum programs can be open and available every open hour. However, investing as little as $15,000 or $20,000 in interactive spaces can allow you to connect with visitors every hour. If located in a high-traffic area, spaces can have fifteen thousand participants or more over a multimonth run.

If your activities are simple with easy, intuitive instructions, the area can be self-directed. For example, visitor services and the education staff can come in to check periodically to observe visitors and restock paper or sharpen colored pencils. Furniture can be as simple as tables, comfortable chairs, or stools that the museum may already own.

Doing these smaller, time-limited projects in-house lets you take small steps toward creating permanent spaces. You can have fun and learn important lessons while building support to tackle large-scale interactivity. In addition, your curators and design staff may be excited to work collaboratively to create a tailored space to activate or capture the essence of an upcoming exhibition or collection.

How Do I Get My Key Leadership on Board?

If you already have a green light to reinstall or create a new family space from your director, senior leadership, or board, then great, you are good to go. But keep your stakeholders close and informed along the way. Regular check-ins at key moments like your vision statement, look and feel decisions, budget con-

ceptual design, and, of course, sign-offs on deliverables will make for fewer surprises and reworking as you near the end.

If you don't have leadership support yet, do you have an advocacy plan? How do you plan to convince the powers that be to give you the green light? One way is your vision and intention statement, which we'll cover next. There are also great resources out there that help you adapt business models for green lighting projects.[1]

Seek internal museum advocates. Start with your immediate director or person you report to up the chain of command and begin to build support. First, you have to know that you have support and sign-off from that person. Establish a need. Do other departments in the museum share that need? How would building the family audience make the museum stronger? Would membership get on board, the marketing department, development team, public programs? If you can pull together a coalition to get behind the idea of new interactive space for families your chances of success go up. Audience evaluation and budget proposals will also be useful in the process, and both are addressed in this chapter. Back up your ideas with evidence and clearly articulate the costs to create extremely compelling arguments for your projects. Once you start gaining traction for the idea across the museum, look for folks who have access to or the ear of the museum director, board members or trustees, or key community museum supporters. The more complete and thoughtful your proposal, the higher the chance of success.

What Is Your Vision?

Have you developed a goals-outcomes-vision document or statement for your reinstalled, refreshed, or new family space? This is an invaluable tool that will be helpful throughout your process. It can be used for funding proposals, attached to the RFPs if you seek an outside designer, or to guide discussion with the in-house design team, it can be the basis of a press release or website copy. See an example of the High Museum's Vision/Intention statement for the new Greene Family Gallery in appendix A.

Here are some things to consider as you create yours:

- Where will your room be located? It should be easy to find. Research shows location plays a big part in how often family spaces in art museums are used.
- Will your room be staffed or not?

One of the things we knew we were going to need was staff and we did have staffing as an operational cost. Staffing could be a big surprise for people. It is a balance between reinforcing, not talking too much, and also trying to find a comfortable place with visitors. We try to support them.

—Cynthia Moreno, Senior Director
of Learning and Engagement,
the Mint Museum, formerly
Director of Education, Speed Art Museum

- Develop a set of emotional goals. How do you want visitors to feel in your space?
- Select a theoretical research base: museum education; art education; creative play; concepts/skills-based learning; social interaction; styles of learning.
- Establish what look and feel you imagine for the space. What's your design vision?
- Draw on child development research.
- Know your audience: identify age ranges for the children in the families and if adults will be independent learners along with families in the interactive space.
- Know your intentions for your audience: identify how you imagine children and adults will interact together in the space: individually, as small groups, as larger groups.
- Will the space be accessible to school groups? This may impact many aspects of your design.
- Vary approaches for different styles of learning.
- Consider intergenerational learning as another dimension of family learning.
- Select an intentional plan for referencing artwork from your collection: referential versus inclusion of original works of art or larger theoretical concepts.
- Select objects or areas of the collections or exhibitions that make a direct connection with the activities.
- Gauge the level of visitor needs: approach visitors in balance with their perceived needs.
- Will your space be high tech, low tech, or something in between?

Create your vision and intention document through an iterative process involving in-house staff, community groups, school groups, if applicable, and, of course, families. Think of it as a learn-as-you-go approach. As you begin to clarify what you want and what you don't want in terms of the feel and spirit of the space, ask others who will use the space to reflect on your thinking.

Get the Community Involved!

Although it takes time and patience, involving the community in your process reaps huge benefits. But who do you involve, why, how, and at what stages? Go back to your vision and intention statement: What kind of experts and audience representation will best get you to your goals? Maximize availability of expertise at all levels: education experts; early childhood learning experts; experience of museum educators; volunteers, teachers; parents; children. Seek expertise in areas of education pedagogy. Sometimes you can even get folks who serve more than one purpose; think of a great design mind in your community who is also the parent of young children; a kindergarten teacher who specializes in a certain field of learning that matches the plans for your space; or a local university professor who teaches about innovation. Be creative and gather a group of six to eight community members who would be willing to spend about a year with you. It's important to do more than ask these advisers to rubber stamp; they need true involvement. By engaging them for about a year, they can be connected to the full process and provide input at key points just like the cross-museum team will. Think about a schedule as you reach out to invite participation. Will you ask them to meet quarterly, bimonthly? Their perspective on the concepts, initial designs, testing, and final designs will make the project stronger.

Once you have settled on the group, host a charrette or community/education focus groups. You'll probably want to do this in the evening or on a weekend because these people likely all have full-time jobs. Serve dinner and wine, if appropriate, and really listen.

NOW MAKE DEFINITE PLANS!
Museum practitioners who have developed one or more family galleries are excellent sources of advice, as is visiting spaces to see how visitors actually use them. Certainly, visiting children's museums and interactive science centers is a good place to start. You can get excellent advice on how to make an interactive that will hold up to constant use from activity designers in these types of museums. We also recommend that you look at spaces and experiences that are not in art museums but attract and hold family visitors' interest in some way that intrigues you. Sometimes these can be activities at local festivals or events or other kinds of destinations. In other words, don't limit your exploration to art museum family spaces. Expand your curiosity. Inspiration is often found in the most unlikely areas.

Do You Have a Comprehensive Evaluation Plan?

Frequently, practitioners think of evaluation as something done at the end of a project. In fact, evaluation is much more useful when planned at the beginning of a project and implemented throughout. This is especially true with family interactive spaces. Think about it. If you wait until everything is finished, then evaluation can only tell you the degree to which you achieved what you wanted. You can't do anything about it. When you use evaluation at the beginning and throughout the process you are able to make changes as you go.

> One of the key benefits of evaluation is how it can be a catalyst to recalibrate your museum's priorities. At the Speed, we used our research to make the case that the location of Art Sparks—the "gem in the basement"—made it consistently hard to find. To dramatically open up Art Sparks and the basement the architects used "acupuncture"—punching holes to let light stream into the lower level. Today Speed visitors can travel to Art Sparks through a bright, spacious concourse.
>
> —Cynthia Moreno, Senior Director of Learning and Engagement, The Mint Museum, formerly Director of Education, Speed Art Museum

First, start by collecting results from studies conducted at other museums. We have gathered many study results in this book, but we don't presume to say this is a comprehensive review of all research. In many cases museums do not publish the results of their needs assessments and formative evaluation. When you contact practitioners for their lessons learned, also ask them about their evaluation process.

Next, engage your staff in conducting some "cheap and cheerful" do-it-yourself front-end and needs assessments. In fact, the process you use to create, review, and revise your vision/intention document should include some sort of needs assessment. Using staff to do this type of evaluation helps to resolve any log jams that might arise within your team. Once your planning process seems to have dissolved into a win-lose conflict, take the problem to your visitors. For example, when a science center was planning an exhibition on health and the human body, one camp felt strongly that graphics and displays of human organs and such should be realistic photos or models. The other camp felt just as strongly that these graphics should be simplified and brightly colored drawings.

The team was at an impasse. We asked the designers to create two treatments, one showing an activity station with emphasis on real models and photos, the other showing the same station with the simplified illustrations and models. We took it to the visitors and asked them to tell us which they preferred and why. Asking "why?" gives you more information than just getting them to vote on their preference. As it turned out, visitors liked aspects of both approaches. They did prefer the realistic photos and models, but they were also attracted to the colorful, more cheerful design approach shown in the other treatment. The designers came up with a blend of the two approaches. The impasse was solved!

> (Piloting/beta testing) really helped us work out any issues with functionality, with communication, with levels of text—those were good things to do. It is still part of renewing the gallery.
>
> —Anne Henderson, Director of Education and Engagement, Frist Art Museum, Nashville, Tennessee

Prototype testing is probably the most important evaluation you can do in this type of project. You can create paper mock-ups of your ideas that give visitors the general idea. Invite them to explore the activity, observe what they do, then talk to them afterward. You don't have to do this with many people to find out what is and isn't working in the idea. Often family activity station ideas are born out of facilitated activities that museum practitioners do with families all the time. Keep testing to figure out if and how you can translate your most successful hands-on activities that you do during special family programs with museum staff guidance, into a self-led activity in your family space.

Remember to have team debriefing sessions after all these evaluation efforts. Although you want to involve as many staff as possible, not just educators, this is sometimes not possible. Be sure to invite staff outside of your department to your debriefing sessions. Write up brief one-page memos of findings and conclusions for people who can't attend your meetings.

Do You Have a Marketing Plan?

Like the evaluation plan, we often leave our thinking about marketing to the end. Perhaps it will be helpful to think of marketing in terms of how you need to keep which people informed of your project.

Consequently, it's important to keep your marketing staff involved in the large team from the start. First of all, this may surprise your marketing staff because we often keep them in the dark until we suddenly need them to get the word out and bring people in. When you include marketing staff throughout the project, they provide excellent guidance and they feel invested, excited, and itching to get the word out about your space. They can help you craft messages to funders and board members in the early stages. By including them early on you give them time to create a range of possible marketing approaches. You can even test some of these approaches during your formative evaluation efforts.

What about the Project Budget?

When we have made presentations on interactive spaces in art museums over the years, the main questions from the audience tend to revolve on the budget. For example, "What was your budget for your space?" or "What should the budget be for a family gallery?" Before answering these questions, we ask all the questions we've asked previously, especially questions about vision, scope, and benefits of the space to visitors. It's not surprising that this is often the first question, because as museum educators we tend to focus on the nuts and bolts of a project. So, if you jumped down to this section without addressing the previous questions, please go back and do the challenging but critically important thinking before dealing with the nuts and bolts.

You can create exciting and innovative spaces on a shoestring budget. Having a huge budget does not assure your space will rock your visitors' world. It is also critical that you include your development and fundraising team in your early planning sessions.

> Time, money, quality. You may not be able to do it all. Allocate time, funds, and development for creativity.
>
> —Patricia Rodewald, former Eleanor McDonald Storza Director of Education, High Museum of Art, Atlanta, Georgia

Carefully consider the main budget buster: technology. We've noticed that museum practitioners often think they have to infuse their family gallery space with cutting-edge technology. Funders and board members also are known to think this is a require-

ment. The reason often goes something like: "But the kids won't come unless we have technology!"

Our experience and research finding suggest it's not that simple. Back in 2001, when computer/digital technology was not in every hand and home, a group of preteens was asked about what they expected to do at the museum. Surprisingly, digital technology, such as playing a game on computers, fell to the bottom of the list of choices. We told them that adults thought that a museum had to have high-tech interactives to interest them. One boy said, "Well, they are wrong!"[2] Our conversation further revealed that they wanted to do and see "cool stuff" they couldn't see anywhere else. Even twenty years ago young people saw a difference between the uniqueness of seeing real objects and playing computer games that were similar to games they played at home or school.

Adults weighed in on this subject too. One woman said she spent enough time on the computer at work and she didn't want to do that during her museum visit. Parents often said they found it hard enough to keep their children off the computer or away from the television. They were hoping the museum would help them help their children unplug for a while. In addition, children need multiple opportunities to practice small and large motor skills outside of a digital environment.

When the High Museum conducted visitor research for the current reinstallation of the Greene Family Learning Gallery in 2016 the question of technology was explored.[3] Interactive activities using what the museum deemed "magical technology" were tested and visitors were invited to use sticky notes to tell the High what they were looking for in the new space. The second-largest category of answers centered on technology. When staff talked with parents, what we heard was that using technology to allow for creativity, engagement, and fun was welcome, but they preferred we stay away from screens that were similar to what the children can get at home—iPads, mobile phones, and tablets, for example.

So, a family interactive gallery doesn't have to be absent of all digital technology. It means that it's not an absolute necessity. Technology should only be used when it suits your end goal and best serves the idea's execution. Just remember that including digital technology will greatly increase the budget in the design, fabrication, maintenance, and periodic replacement of hardware and software.

There are a few rules of thumb that we use in the consideration of digital technology in family interactive galleries.

1. Is digital technology the *only* and *best* way that the experience you are planning can be accomplished?

   For example, if the same experience can be achieved with a no-tech or low-tech solution then that's your answer.

   So, at the beginning of our space and still to this day—use the right tool for the job. Is technology the right tool to accomplish the job? Are you using technology as a bell and a whistle or because it best presents a big idea?

   —Anne Henderson, Director of Education and Engagement, Frist Art Museum, Nashville, Tennessee

2. Is the digital interface an experience that visitors *cannot find anywhere* else?

   If your tech idea is similar to something already on smartphone and tablet apps then it doesn't pass the "uniqueness" test. Of course, there are always exceptions. Maybe the interface is familiar but the content or approach is unique.

3. Does your institution have the *capacity* to *maintain* digital technology?

   Things with moving parts and electronics that are subjected to heavy use by visitors are going to break down. They will need repair, rebooting, and replacement. If you are not able to service hardware and software in-house then your budget needs to accommodate hiring outside repair and service.

   If you can't take care of it, don't get it.

   —Cynthia Moreno, Senior Director of Learning and Engagement, the Mint Museum, formerly Director of Education, Speed Art Museum

4. How quickly will your technology interactive go out of date?

   You don't have to be that old to have witnessed how quickly newer technology eclipses what seemed new yesterday. Also, what seems like the next new thing might not make it very long. Does anyone remember Betamax? Given the time it takes to thoughtfully design, fabricate, and install a family gallery the chances of your technology design becoming obsolete is high.

5. A little bit of high technology goes a long way.

   Unless you are a museum dedicated to high technology then you can employ a light touch in the inclusion of technology in your family gallery. Remember that you can be truly unique and not use any high-tech experiences. Then you can market your experience as a unique opportunity for the family to unplug, unwind, and reconnect to each other.

Ask for Budget Options from Designers and Fabricators

Designers and fabricators tend toward the best or highest-end solution for your needs. Don't be shy in asking them to provide two or three different budget approaches. Then your team can consider the options in light of your vision and outcomes.

Make your plan and be willing to change it. You have to have flexibility.

—Anne Henderson, Director of Education and Engagement, Frist Art Museum, Nashville, Tennessee

Create a Budget with Built-in Flexibility

There are so many unanticipated expenses during all phases of a family gallery project. Here are a few considerations that will help you weather the planned-for and the unexpected.

1. Include a sustainability/renewal budget from the inception of the project. Create an annual line-item budget that keeps the gallery sufficiently fresh, appealing, and up-to-date. When you budget for renewal of specific aspects of your space, create a renewal or refreshment schedule and put those dates on your calendar. Don't keep putting it off.
2. Establish a contingency fund. It's important to have a contingency line in the budget. Usually for a large project that involves both design and fabrication you would want a range of from 5 to 10 percent set aside.
3. Managing the budget is critical. It might seem obvious, but a project of this scale is bigger than what we do in our day-to-day education work. The invoices start coming in fast and furious so it is critical to have a system to monitor the spending against the budget almost daily. Constantly monitor invoicing and expenditures.

You want renewal built into the initial planning. It's huge.

—Anne Henderson, Director of Education and Engagement, Frist Art Museum, Nashville, Tennessee

If you incorporate it into your fund-raising efforts you will have allocated dollars. If you have an endowment then it's going to be protected. If it is fee-based—you have a business model.

—Patricia Rodewald, former Eleanor McDonald Storza Director of Education, High Museum of Art, Atlanta, Georgia

Who Will Design and Build Your Family Gallery?

Certainly, design of the space will be driven by the vision statement and outcomes you created at the beginning of your development process. Whether you use an outside designer or fabricator to take your vision to a reality depends on several factors. If someone in your institution has experience in designing such spaces, then you are in luck. If your in-house designer does not have expertise in designing interactives that can withstand heavy use with grace, then you may need an outside codesigner. Or your in-house designer may not be interested or have the time to work on your project. If there is a children's museum or science center in your area you might find the expertise you need in their design team. Otherwise, there are many good independent designers and design firms. Sometimes museums use an outside designer but are able to fabricate the designs in-house. Usually, museums use outside fabricators because the skills needed to build structures that can withstand heavy use by visitors are quite specialized.

If you are seeking an outside design firm, do your research to create your short list of designers you want to consider. To build your list think about what you loved in the spaces you visited in preparation for this project. Who designed the places you were inspired by the most? Ask art museum colleagues with family spaces you admire who designed their space. Also consider designers of interesting spaces in other types of institutions. Winnow down your list to the three or four top candidates who will receive your RFP (see the next section for more information on RFPs).

Some design firms also do the fabrication, the building of your design, although you may need to contract with a separate fabrication company. Again, recommendations from colleagues are a good way to find the group that best fits your needs. Your designers may also have fabricators they have worked with in the past.

In any case, select a designer and fabricator who have a common desire to collaborate with and listen to you, listen to each other, and meet budgets and deadlines. It is important to include this expectation in the RFP. Be sure to add to the fabrication contract that you will need postbuild customer service. This involves warranties and maintenance service for several years after opening your space.

You need enough money so that your designer and fabricator have direct contact with each other. The conversation between the fabricator and designer is really important.

—Julia Forbes, Shannon Landing Amos Head of Museum Interpretation, High Museum of Art, Atlanta, Georgia

Once you have selected your designer and fabricator, establish lines of communication between all parties including your project manager, designer, and fabricator. Establish shared, documented expectations between project manager, designer, and fabricator. Your museum project manager must create a detailed timeline and a process for consistent and frequent check-in. The check-ins will most frequently be done through a project management software (your designer and fabricators may already have one in place) but also schedule regular face-to-face meetings or virtual meetings. Have a clear agenda for each of these meetings.

Test all materials for durability over time and unexpected usages by visitors. You can do this type of testing yourself in your project evaluation plan or include it in the fabricator's contract. Be sure to include testing for those with various accessibility considerations. But do it!

What Is an RFP and How Do You Create the Best One?

An RFP is the acronym for request for proposal. This document is created by the museum and sent to the designers you would like to submit proposals. Many RFPs are so general or vague that the proposals you get back from designers will be so different that it's impossible to meaningfully compare them. It's no surprise then that the better the RFP, the better the proposal. Even if you plan to use your in-house designer, you need to create this type of document. Check out appendix B for a successful example of an RFP.

There are many resources online for writing an RFP[4] and you should definitely consider those guidelines. This will help you write a "good" RFP. However, if you want to find the best designer for your project you want to write a "great" RFP. Your vision and intention statement (described previously) is an essential first step to creating a document that will inspire your designers. Although there is basic information that has to go into an RFP, in the sections where you describe the project and your vision for the project, you have an opportunity to tell a compelling story. If these sections don't make you excited to get started, then how can it stir the creative juices of your designer? If you use a separate fabrication firm, then your designer can help you with the development of a fabrication RFP, if you include that feature in your contract with the designer.

> Designers need to understand your look and feel and how people move through space. We wanted it to have the same aesthetics as the building, and yet also wanted it to have a high quality (personal) aesthetic so it was asking children to step up to an aesthetic—and not asking adults to step down.
>
> —Anne Henderson, Director of Education and Engagement, Frist Art Museum, Nashville, Tennessee

Other Thoughts to Consider

This section provides some final thoughts as you create and implement your vision for a family space. We've added a checklist in appendix C for a bit of extra help.

- Establish a balance between the types of activities designed on several levels. Have a mix of things that can be done alone and those that need two or more people. Depending on if and how you plan to staff the space, consider how many stations will need facilitation by staff, teacher, or parent and what experiences can be done independently, without anyone helping.

> I think you've got to have some sense about flow and how the space may be used. So in the early design phases you may not know. It affects your changes. Some stations are more popular than others and you get logjams and so you need to have that flexibility built into the space. What are ways I can design it so I can open the space or add to the space?
>
> —Anne Henderson, Director of Education and Engagement, Frist Art Museum, Nashville, Tennessee

- Balance also involves the "heat" levels across activities. Some activities are high energy. For example, visitors may create more noise or physical activity in a station. While you want to create some "hot" or high activity zones, you don't want the whole space to be high activity. Balance the heat with some warm and cool zones. Warm activities might involve several people or a small degree of noise while cool experiences are reflective and calming. Make a type of map of your spaces so you have a visual representation of your heat levels. See appendix D for an example of a heat map created for the 2005 iteration of the Greene Family Learning Gallery at the High Museum.

> We care passionately about balance. We can feel if two "hot" things are put next to each other.
>
> —Gwendolyn Kelly, former Project Manager, Speed Art Museum, Louisville, Kentucky

- How do you feel about messes? We are referring to the collective, institutional "you." For example, you may be fine with seeing art materials spread around but someone else in your museum may find it exceedingly annoying. As you plan your experiences for families, consider the level of mess your museum can tolerate. For example, will you use consumable materials such as paper, pencils, markers, and other media? This will create a mess but messes are not bad things. They are only a problem if you have not planned for it. Do you know whose job it will be to do the straightening and restocking? What happens if that person is out and you have high visitation that day? Think about weekend visitation and availability of staff.
- Avoid gratuitous interactivity. Once when testing an interactive zone for a science center, one of the activities involved moving a light beam forward and back. After watching visitors use this station and talking with them about the experience, we had a conversation with the in-house designer. What, exactly, did moving the light mean? How did moving it help the visitor understand the scientific concept presented? The designer said, "It doesn't mean anything and it doesn't explain the concept. We just thought people might want to move something." That is the definition of gratuitous interactivity.

> We aren't big flippers and button pushers. And so we kept asking two questions, What are they actually doing? What connections are they making?
>
> —Cynthia Moreno, Senior Director of Learning and Engagement, the Mint Museum, formerly Director of Education, Speed Art Museum

- Will your space accommodate school groups? Some family spaces are off-limits to school groups while others design specifically for this audience. Be clear about your intentions and design accordingly. Large groups with fewer adults have implications on staffing, wear and tear, as well as physical spacing.
- Where will you store supplies and cleaning materials? Will this area be directly accessible to the family gallery or are stations designed to store the materials and supplies?
- Consider the shelf life of your family space. Do you plan to completely renovate every few years or replace individual stations periodically? Create a clear plan for how the space will evolve over time. High-tech devices will need replacement as will the much-loved and quickly soiled puppets. We recommend having replacements available at the start.
- Consider the ergonomics within your design. Because this is a family space you will have big people and little people. If you want adults to stay engaged with their children then provide comfortable seating and sufficient space for "bigs" as well as "littles."
- Build to industrial standards without looking industrial. This might be one the hardest things for art museums to do.

People are not kind to interactive spaces. So you do need to choose things that withstand well-intentioned use and abuse.

—Anne Henderson, Director of Education and Engagement, Frist Art Museum, Nashville, Tennessee

A while back, a contemporary art museum created a space for families and school groups where artists created experiential, hands-on art. For example, children could walk through a door, touch works specially designed for touching, and sit on or crawl through spaces. Although these creations were unique and full of wonder, they lasted about two weeks before hinges fell off, pieces broke, and sharp edges appeared that threatened safety. The artists had amazing ideas, but they did not have experience in fabricating something that could withstand heavy use. This is where they could have benefited from a collaboration between the artist and a children's museum fabricator.

- To ensure you've covered all your bases and are considering a wide range of learning styles and abilities, a simple chart can be a useful tool. In appendix E you'll find an example that the design firm Roto and the High Museum created for the Greene Family Learning Gallery 2018 installation. We called it our "experience matrix." It tracks every activity in the room against a wide range of variables like ages, our goals for the space, inclusivity, and skill building.
- Host museum staff and boards of trustee meetings in the interactive space right after it opens and periodically throughout the time it is on view. Consider inviting community groups to meet in the space. Give them a brief introduction and a tour, then let them have their regular business meeting that day. Have a special family event in your space for ride-share and taxi drivers. They are great sources of "what to do" information in your city. If they have a personal experience with their family then they will be your greatest ambassadors.

So now it's time to get started. Build your team, do your homework and research, write your vision and intention statement, develop your goals, invite in your community, craft your budget, and start planning for front-end evaluation. Good luck! It will be hard work, frustrating at times, take long hours, sweat, and tears, but it will all be worth it when you see all those families gathered together bonding and making memories in your space as they learn together about art and themselves.

NOTES

1. Fast Company has great resources. Accessed May 5, 2021, at https://www.fastcompany.com/3032692/how-to-get-the-green-light-for-your-big-idea; *10 Things to do Before Greenlighting a New Project.* Accessed May 5, 2021, at https://earlygrowthfinancialservices.com/10-things-to-do-before-green-lighting-a-new-project/.
2 Adams and Contini, 2001.
3. Ancelet, 2016.
4. For example, https://blog.bit.ai/how-to-write-an-rfp/. Accessed May 5, 2021.

REFERENCES

Adams, M., and H. Contini. *Front-End Evaluation Study, San Diego Natural History Museum New Exhibition Design Process* (unpublished technical report). Annapolis, MD: Institute for Learning Innovation, 2001.
Ancelet, J. *Art Lab Evaluation Report for the High Museum of Art* (unpublished technical report). Davidsonville, MD: Audience Focus, 2016.

Our intention was to fill this book with key research findings, lessons learned in the field, and tools to help you create a new family interactive space, refresh an existing space, or experiment with temporary spaces in various nooks and crannies throughout the museum. We've provided the "Who" and "What" of family audiences in art museums based on research over the past few decades. We've given checklists and suggestions for the "How" of developing family interactive experiences. We want to take one last opportunity to stress the importance of spending the majority of your initial planning time on the "Why" of these spaces and to revisit your work on this area frequently throughout the development and operation of your interactive spaces. This involves fully articulating why families want the interactive experience in the museum and why you, as practitioners, are putting in all this effort. In our experience, we find that museum practitioners, well, humans in general, tend to jump over this part. We can tell if this is the case just by walking through family interactive spaces created without a clearly articulated vision and application of the values and benefits of the space.

We subtitled the book *Creating Curiosity, Wonder, and Play* because these are the key ways families value their experiences in the museum. This, for us, is the core answer to the "Why?" question. But it's not enough to want that for your family visitors. You, as museum practitioners, need to embody these concepts. Because if we don't embody these ideas as practitioners, we cannot authentically create them for our visitors. To create vital spaces filled with curiosity, wonder, and play, these must be more than words. They must be in you and your team from the start of the project.

CURIOSITY

At the core of curiosity is a desire to learn or know about anything and everything. How inquisitive are you and your team? Inquisitiveness requires effort. Do you truly want to find out why visitors behave as they do in your museum? Or do you really, deep down

Figure E.1. Family working together at Community Tree, Greene Family Learning Gallery, 2018, ©CatMax, High Museum of Art. Used by permission, CatMax Photography

inside, just want the visitors to do what you want them to do? Curiosity plays out when you pay close attention to what families do, when you listen to what they want, and when you figure out what they need, even if the visitors don't realize it (figure E.1).

During Marianna's mini-sabbatical at the Isabella Stewart Gardner Museum during summer 2014 she decided to just kick back and hang out with families in the museum. It took some effort to not have an agenda or to pepper the families with questions, but she was amazed at how quickly she was willing to let go and how much she enjoyed just being with the families and not doing. One of the most treasured discoveries relates to the sublime joy that she found following pure curiosity and was recounted in her third blog post, musing about her time at the Gardner:

I am continually fascinated by what draws children's attention and this week's visits were no exception. Typically, it is not what educators tend to include on tours. For example, Suzie was first taken with the missing head on a statue in the courtyard. Throughout the visit she commented on how many statues were missing heads and arms. This caused us all to heighten our attention to what was missing. When we passed along a hallway to go upstairs, she paused at a niche housing several stone and marble heads along with a sculpture missing all limbs and the head. She said, "Oh, so this must be where they keep the heads" and calmly walked on.

Children frequently stumped us all with their insightful questions that we couldn't answer. When that happened, all of us, adults and children, got involved in the conversation, equally contributing bits and pieces of what we knew and speculating on all the possible answers. Yes, I could analyze these interchanges and point to how they are modeling critical thinking, good inquiry, and how children need to see that no one has all the answers, but I'm not. They were just beautiful moments of people coming together and puzzling out something. I want to leave it at that.[1]

Curiosity can also be experimentation. Break some rules, try new things, evaluate, test, pull it off the floor and try again, and again, and again. Museum educators tend to see things through our own practitioner's lens. Move your ideas and assumptions to the background and press the mute button for awhile. How can you elegantly marry your desires for the interactive space with what families value?

What are *you* curious about? Curiosity is a rare and novel thing. Treasure it and develop ways to make it a constant part of your practice!

Figure E.2. Child playing in Wonder Cove, Greene Family Learning Gallery, 2018. Used by permission, Julia Forbes, photographer

WONDER

To wonder is to be astonished. It's a feeling of surprise mingled with admiration, caused by something beautiful, unexpected, unfamiliar, or inexplicable (figure E.2).

True story. Picture a two-and-a-half-year-old boy with his mother walking into a museum gallery filled floor to ceiling with sixteenth-century paintings and decorative arts. He gives a long, drawn out "Wow" in true admiration of just being in the space. He was too young to understand that he was in the presence of some true masterworks. He was just in the fullness of wonder. This was an expression he offered several times throughout the museum visit, but he didn't express it everywhere. He exercised discrimination.

Sometimes when we work in museums all the time we stop seeing with eyes of wonder. How can nurturing your personal state of wonder be helpful to your practice in the museum? What would happen if you saw what is so familiar to you with a different set of eyes, from a different perspective? Put yourself in your visitors' shoes and stand back as a slew of surprising ideas and "ah-ha's" come to the surface. When you and your team visit other interactive spaces, be the visitor. Better yet, accompany a few young children or entire families to the museum. Leave your museum hat and your agenda at the door. Revel fully in *your* inner child.

To be in a state of wonder is a marvelous thing. The now trite term "awesome" comes to mind, as in full to bursting with awe. To be in a state of awe means you experience something powerful, even overwhelming. But allowing yourself to be overwhelmed by wonder can result in feelings of uncertainty. That is powerful too. It's OK not to know and do it anyway; trust the process.

What lights *you* up? If the experiences you plan for families don't "ring your bell," don't do it.

PLAY

Play has multiple connotations: to move lightly and quickly; to occupy or busy oneself; and to amuse oneself. It can mean to engage in active exercise or to frolic and to make believe. To be cooperative and to be part of a team is another form of play. We get that children need to play (figure E.3). What is less understood is that adults need to play too.

We want to make two key points here:

1. You, an adult and a museum practitioner, have to tap into your sense of playfulness to create playful experiences for families—you can't fake this; and

Figure E.3. Child playing in Art Lab, High Museum of Art, 2016. Used by permission, Sarah Schleuning, photographer

2. The play experiences you create for families need a sense of intentionality behind them. Otherwise how is your interactive experience unique?

The Playful Museum Practitioner

Play is an activity engaged in for enjoyment and recreation, especially for children. This is a typical definition, but we think it's more. Play is not just for kids, it's serious fun, and adults benefit from play, too. Dr. Stuart Brown from the National Institute of Play says: "Play is something done for its own sake. It's voluntary, it's pleasurable, it offers a sense of engagement, it takes you out of time. And the act itself is more important than the outcome."[2]

You have to *be* playful in order to *create* playfulness. So make sure your team has time to have fun together. Make play part of your brainstorming, your planning in your community meetings, and your visitor testing. Infuse the process of creating amazing family experience with a sense of playfulness. If it's not fun for you, why do it?

Intentionality Behind the Play

For us, for play to have genuine value for families in your museum it requires being intentional about the nature of that play experience.

Is your museum just a "sexy backdrop"[3] for play? If families can do the same thing anywhere—a park, a play space in an airport or shopping mall, at home, or in the car—then the play at your museum is not intentional. Art museums are not children's museums or history museums or science museums. The main challenge is to create a unique play experience in your museum. This is what we mean by "intentionality." This even *plays* into how you design your space. What is your aesthetic? How can you intentionally make your space look like it belongs in *your* museum rather than any museum?

You as the creator must have intentionality behind the play opportunities you create. Think about what kind of play you want to develop. Our research has shown that families value bonding and shared meaning-making. So, while it's fine for children to play and be entertained in a safe place with caregivers doing adult stuff (catching up, drinking coffee, etc.), the play in the art museum can be different in quality and value, taking the whole family to a deeper place. The museum play environment should be about family engagement and play together. Families create imaginative play experiences; they do this together naturally.

Where can you find the sense of playfulness in your museum? Think of fifty different ways to bring that sense to the forefront!

NOTES

1. Art Museum Teaching blogsite. Accessed June 30, 2021, at https://artmuseumteaching.com/2014/07/15/falling-in-love-with-your-visitors/.
2 "Play Doesn't End With Childhood: Why Adults Need Recess Too" on *All Things Considered*, August 6, 2014. Accessed June 30, 2021, at https://www.npr.org/sections/ed/2014/08/06/336360521/play-doesnt-end-with-childhood-why-adults-need-recess-too.
3. Thanks to Patricia Rodewald for using this terminology to wake us up!

Sample Vision and Intention Statement for the Greene Family Learning Gallery, 2018

Greene Family Learning Gallery
Vision & Intention Statement

We want family visitors to feel:
- *welcome* and a sense of belonging
- *curious*
- *creative, imaginative, playful*
- *relaxed* that their kids can be kids
- a stronger *connection* between parents & children
- *empowered* to visit the Museum with their children
- *grateful* for the memories and family time
- *motivated* to return often

Working Title: Curiosity, Wonder, & Play: Thinking Like an Artist

Audience

Families – adults with children ages 3 to 8 years old, intergenerational groups. This means that we want to address the needs and interests of the whole family in the same space.

School Groups – on a scheduled and facilitated basis in small groups (12-15 students)

Role of the Space in the Overall Museum Visit

In the past we positioned of the family galleries as a launching pad to the permanent collection. However, we now know from research that most families use the family gallery as a last stop. Many parents say it is the "carrot" at the end of the visit, a way to get the children to first go through the galleries. They also appreciate having a space where they can relax and not have to keep children from touching or being too rambunctious. Sometimes the family gallery visit occurs midway through the museum visit. This makes sense, as it is located in the space that adjoins the two buildings. When family programs are scheduled, the family gallery frequently serves as something to do with the children until the program begins.

Conceptual-Pedagogical Framework

Reggio Emilia–based approach: Reggio Emilia focused on the connections among how children, learning, and life are viewed.

> The child is viewed as capable, independent, inquisitive and innately driven to learn.
> Learning is an experience, not separate from, but deeply rooted in life.
> Life, the world around us, is part of us, open and available for the children to explore and discover, to interact with, naturally.
> This approach involves working, exploring, creating with real materials; discussing options, problem-solving, directing their own play, free to wonder.

Social experience – making memories together
> Work together & parallel play
> Stimulate conversation
> Empower parents to talk with children about art

Participatory, open-ended, not prescribed
Balance Independence (child can do on own/self-evident) with collaborative experiences where s/he needs or wants adults

Design Issues
Reggio Emilia-based design

      Real surfaces/treatments, wood, glass, metal

      Modern, clean, aesthetically refined

      Natural palette

      Children deserved to be surrounded by beautiful things

      Bring the outdoors indoors – see the natural world from inside

      The design of the physical space fosters encounters, communication, and relationships.

      A sense of spaciousness, uncluttered

Visual cues communicate that the space is for everyone. We don't want an obvious "kids" space with over-bright "kid" colors. We want the parents/caregivers to want to come in too, not just for their children.

Universal Design: While we expect that the design with conform with current ADA regulations, we want to go further and consider design for audiences with mixed abilities. For example, some of these children respond well when there are varieties of texture, not every surface is smooth. We find that when we make these accommodations, everyone benefits.

Flexibility: We know that visitors like to see something new when they come and would like to be able to switch out activities in the space ourselves. We envision a schedule for cycling activities through the area. It is possible that we can recycle areas every 1 – 3 years, depending on the type and popularity of the area. We want to explore the design of modular furniture or cases that can be moved easily by educators. If possible, we'd like our design team to help us plan for change, helping us set up a schedule for changing areas, and giving us some ideas to begin working on once the new installation opens.

Two Spaces: We have 2 equal size spaces with a wide dividing hallway (see floor plan) and each space has two walls of windows. One space (the current family gallery) overlooks the piazza and the other overlooks the street. It is possible to partially or fully block the light in the spaces. We envision that at least one of the two spaces will have a lot of natural light.

We are leaning towards having two different types of experiences in the two spaces but want our designer to explore this issue with us. Some of our questions about the design of the two spaces are: What do we gain or lose by treating these spaces as separate with a different design and/or content approach in each? What do we gain or lose by thinking of the spaces as a continuation of the same approach? What about the hallway? How can we bridge the two spaces even if they are two different approaches? It is possible that we can spill out into the hallway to some degree.

Content Puddles
We realize that there are other content areas that we have not listed here. We will rely on the designer to expand our thinking about content and this list can start that conversation.

Architecture: We would like to have an activity/area(s) that address architecture as an art form and two architects of the Museum, Renzo Piano & Richard Meier. We are also interested in ways to connect the built environment with the everyday life of kids and adults.

Sculpture: We have found that building things, in small scale such as blocks, and large scale such as big shapes that can be linked, is enjoyable for all children, as well as adults. Using seemingly disparate parts to make something new is also an interesting challenge for visitors. Construction, as well as destruction (taking things apart) of the built shape, is equally interesting. We would like to explore ways of creating in three dimensions in both large and/or small-scale projects.

Think like an artist: We acknowledge that the creative process varies widely across artists and that there is no one way to thinking like an artist. We would like to explore ways that we can authentically explore the creative process. Some ideas we've generated relate to how artists think about and use light, the artist's process, why artists create, ways to immerse children in the art, work with local artists, incorporating movement/kinesthetic in exploration of art

Visual Literacy: Our research suggests that adults want/need more experiences that assist them in close looking and making meaning from art for their children (and themselves it appears). We want to reach beyond the common approach of identifying elements of art (e.g., line, shape, color, texture). The elements of art merely tools we use to better understand a work of art, not an end itself. We would like to help families develop a shared language for how they talk about art. Visual literacy includes but is not limited to:

- Storytelling and narrative: How we can tell a story without words in visual images, sound, and movement
- Critical thinking: How we use the skills of inference, compare/contrast, multiple perspectives, and sequencing to make sense of art
- Ambiguity: How we don't always fully understand what something "means" but we can still appreciate and enjoy the experience of not knowing and that we can have different interpretations of the same work

Some of the ways we have been thinking about the two spaces:

Space 1	**Space 2**
Modular/flexible activity areas	Immersive
Able for staff to change areas out	Addresses Big ideas
Able to cover or open windows for light/no light	Community-based
	Families to do open-ended things
Project-based activities with prompts and challenges	Artist environment – such as, artist-in-residence program and/or commissioned art
Engage in inquiry, discovery	Have group/child-adult community projects
	Installations that gradually emerge over time, you are part of the art - participatory
	Artistic play-scape

Other Issues

Use of Museum Collections: While we want to reference the main collection areas in the family spaces, we do not plan to use objects from the collections in the space. We are open to the idea of an artist commissions for the space and/or audience-created works.

Use of Technology: We are open to the use or non-use of technology in the family space. We know that some parents appreciate coming to the museum to "unplug" their children. We know that we don't want to have iPads or other commonly-available technology. If we do have technology it should be something that visitors cannot do or see elsewhere, e.g. magical, immersive, unexpected. Of course, the type and amount of technology will be dependent on the project budget.

Use of Museum Staff in the Space: The current family gallery is not staffed, with the exception of volunteers and educators walking through the gallery periodically to tidy up. We are open to creating a space that requires staffing but will need to explore the budget and volunteer management implications of that decision.

Use of Make & Take Art Activities: We lean towards an "non-consumables" experience, meaning we are not inclined to have traditional, individual, studio art making activities as we have multiple studio spaces and provide frequent opportunities for families to make and take art projects. We have found that children are not as attached as their adults to the things they make. It also creates a different level of staffing to be sure that supplies are stocked and paper has a way of finding itself on the floor. We also want to work towards a more sustainable space. We realize that a community art project might involve the use of consumables and are open to that for a specified length of time. The difference here is that what visitors do in a community art project is not taken home.

Design Approach

The Museum views the 50th anniversary of the family gallery program as an opportunity to expand its thinking about the family experience in order to create a unique and highly meaningful experience for our visitors. The ideal design firm will provide a good fit with the Museum's internal project team in spirit, pedagogy, aesthetics, and working approach.

- We want to create a unique and highly meaningful experiences for families, and we want a designer who will push us to think in new ways. How would you start the thinking process?

- We recognize and respect the place of the designer as the key creative partner. At the same time, the Museum's internal project team (about 5 people) wants to participate in the development of the gallery. To this end, please give us an idea of how you might work with us. How do you like to work with museum teams? What do see as the benefits and drawbacks of this type of collaboration?

- We want a space that serves our families and provides a unique, magical, and unexpected experience. In other words, we don't want to replicate what is going on elsewhere. What questions do we need to be asking? Where should we look for inspiration outside of the museum field? What would you encourage us to read, observe, or do as part of the preparation for working together?

- We are struggling with how to address the needs and interests of different ages while still serving the whole family. How would you begin to help us solve this problem?

Sample Request for
Proposal for Outside Designers

Greene Family Learning Gallery Request for Proposal

Introduction:

The High Museum of Art, a division of the Robert W. Woodruff Arts Center, Inc. (Museum) has had a dedicated interactive space for families to learn, play, and explore since 1968. The reinstallation of an expanded Greene Family Learning Gallery in October 2018 offers the Museum the opportunity not only to celebrate this fifty year commitment, but more importantly to re-envision our relationship with Atlanta's families. It is our goal to be a leader in the Southeast in programming designed especially for children and their adult caregivers.

The High's new mantra is Growth, Inclusivity, Collaboration, and Connectivity. These important concepts run through the DNA of the Museum and its staff. We are seeking a designer who will embrace our mantra and challenge us in new ways; a team that can work with us to help us secure the family audience as a central focus. To make the High Museum of Art an essential place for our community, where children and adults can engage together in informal learning, intergenerational communication, and play.

Background:

Past family space installations include:
- 1974-78: *The City*, the urban experience used to teach about the basic elements of art.
- 1983-88: *Sensation*, explored the five senses through arts, science, and technology.
- 1988-93: *Spectacles*, in which nationally recognized artists were commissioned to create interactive installations that dealt with different aspects of the arts.
- 2005-present: *Greene Family Learning Gallery*, the first named space for interactive family installations; installation focused on creative play.

In 2011, the Museum participated in a four-year research study on how families learn in art museum family spaces. This impressive body of research was funded by the Institute of Museum and Library Services (IMLS). Two key findings that will help inform the new design include: 1) the concept of "creative play" is one of the keys to the success of an interactive space, and 2) families highly value these types of spaces for the opportunity to create shared memories. (See attached Executive Summary)

In 2016, the Museum conducted a study to experiment and test activities and concepts for the new Greene Family Learning Gallery. It was also an opportunity to learn from family visitors about what they would like to experience in such a space or setting. The findings of this study support the IMLS study as well as provide specific insight into what types of experiences resonate most with families at the Museum. (See attached study overview)

In 2017, the Museum brought together specialists in different aspects of education, early learning, design-thinking, accessibility and special needs from the Atlanta community for a brainstorm around the new space. These community members will be invaluable partners in testing our design concepts.

Because the Greene Family Learning Gallery has been so popular with families, the institution has committed to doubling its space. The additional space is the same size as the original gallery and directly across a wide and frequently traveled public hallway. The hallway, and ways to link the two spaces, should be considered part of the design challenge. (See attached floor plan)

The Project:

The Museum is seeking a designer or design firm (sometimes referred to as "Respondent") to work together with the Museum's internal team to conceive and develop a plan for reinstallation of the expanded Greene Family Learning Gallery. Fabrication will be handled through a separate RFP process. If Respondent is a design/build firm, the Museum is open to considering a combined proposal upon prior notice.

The new installation of the Greene Family Learning Gallery must achieve the goals outlined in the Vision & Intention document (attached). Our current working title and driving focus is: "Thinking Like An Artist."

Requirements:
- Travel to Atlanta approximately four times during the development of the project to work with the Museum team
- Present the design concept to Museum leadership for review and comment
- Assist Museum team in identifying specific ideas or approaches for concept/prototype testing
  - Provide necessary sketches or paper mock-ups. (Museum staff will conduct the testing)
- Present final design drawings and necessary specifications for inclusion in a separate request for proposal for fabrication of the new Greene Family Learning Gallery

Expectations & Deliverables:

Proposals must be submitted by April 14, 2017 at 12:00 pm EST via email to:

ADD YOUR DETAILS HERE

Submit any questions you have to Ms. Forbes (address above) via email by March 20, 2017 at 12:00pm EST. All those sent an RFP invitation will receive all answers to all questions.

Proposals will be evaluated by a Museum selection committee and notification will be made on or before May 1, 2017.

Proposal must include:

1. Firm Information
- Name of firm
- Complete address
- Contact person
- Telephone number
- Fax number
- Website URL
- E-mail address

2. Qualifications & Personnel
Provide a brief, general statement of qualifications that supports selection of your firm for this project.
Personnel
  a. List the personnel who would be committed to this project, identifying their role, outlining their experience in projects similar to the project proposed in this RFP.
References

    a. Provide the name and phone number of a minimum of two clients with whom you have worked on similar projects.

<u>Special Design Concerns</u>
    b. Explain how your firm ensures compliance with the Americans with Disabilities Act (ADA) as well as integrates Universal Design principles. Provide examples.
    c. Efficient energy usage is a priority of the Museum. Describe how your firm incorporates this aspect of design into its work. Provide examples.

3. Costs

Provide a "lump sum" fee and payment schedule for services in submitted proposal. Include an itemized breakdown of "lump sum" fee, which includes charges for design, conceptual design drawings, fabrication drawings, travel, and other such items required to complete this project and include an hourly or per item rate for design services that may be over and above the scope of work indicated in this proposal. The designer/design firm's price proposal for this project shall be irrevocable for one hundred twenty (120) calendar days from the proposal due date. This period may be extended by written mutual agreement between the Museum and designer/design firm.

Attachments to the RFP:

- High Museum of Art Greene Family Learning Gallery Vision & Intention Statement
- A floor plan of the current and expanded Greene Family Learning Gallery
- Executive Summaries of the IMLS-Funded Research Study on Family Learning in Art Museums conducted by the High Museum in 2011
    - Motivation, Use, Value study available at www.artmuseumfamilyspaces.org
    - Longitudinal Family Case Study www.artmuseumfamilyspaces.org
- Highlights of 2016 Art Lab Study: Full study available at:
    http://www.audiencefocus.com/us/pdf/HighMuseum.ArtLab.StudyResults.V1%20with%20TOC.pdf

Project Timeline:

May 1, 2017
- Select designer

May - June 2017
- Designer makes initial site visit to begin process
- Designer meetings and idea generation (on-site and virtual) with Museum's internal team
- Designer presents initial concepts to Museum's team & leadership

July-September 2017
- Designer and High Museum staff select specific concepts or approaches for concept/prototype testing (Museum conducts testing)

October-December 2017
- Designer presents final design to Museum's team, leadership, and Woodruff Arts Center (WAC) leadership
- Museum & WAC approve final design
- Museum drafts and releases a request for proposal for construction/fabrication for new Greene Family Learning Gallery

January 2018
- Select company to lead construction/fabrication of Greene Family Learning Gallery

February - September 2018
- Off-site fabrication

June - September 2018
- On-site construction and installation

October 2018
- Expanded Greene Family Learning Gallery opens to the public

Documentation:

Following selection of Designer, Museum and Designer will mutually agree to proceed in good faith toward negotiation and execution of a definitive agreement, which will provide for the specific terms of the project described above and contain other provisions standard and customary for agreements of this type, including but not limited to insurance and indemnification. In addition, Museum will be granted ownership rights to all drawings produced by Designer for this project upon payment of services. Copyright will be jointly owned by Museum and Designer.

Proposal Acceptance:

The Museum's selection committee will judge each Respondent based upon its understanding of the responses received from Respondent and will conduct a fair, impartial, and comprehensive evaluation of all responses. If applicable, a contract will be awarded, taking into consideration the best interests of the Museum. The criteria for selecting a Respondent may include, but is not limited to, some or all of the following:

a. Ability, capacity, and skill of Respondent to perform the requirements described herein.
b. Performance level standards and commitments provided by Respondent.
c. Fee structure.
d. Character, integrity, reputation, judgment, experience, and efficiency of Respondent.
e. Quality of Respondent's performance on prior projects.
f. Such other information that may be secured and that has a bearing on the decision to award the contract.

After review of all factors, terms and conditions, including price, the Museum's selection committee will make a recommendation to its leadership, which reserves the right to accept or reject any and all proposals, in whole or in part, received as a result of this RFP; to waive minor irregularities; or to negotiate with all responsible proposers, in any manner necessary, to serve the best interest of the Museum. Further, the Museum reserves the right to make a whole award, multiple awards, a partial award, or no award at all.

Confidentiality:

The information contained in this RFP is confidential and proprietary. This RFP is provided for the exclusive use of the Respondent and copies shall not be made available to any other party without written consent from the Museum. All proposals and supporting documentation shall become the property of the Museum and will not be returned.

Incurred Expenses:

The Museum will not be responsible for any costs incurred by any vendor/firm in preparation and submittal of a proposal in this RFP process.

Checklist of Tasks for Development of Interactive Family Spaces

CHECKLIST OF TASKS FOR INTERACTIVE FAMILY GALLERIES

Common experiences and practices were identified across the focus interactive gallery sites. In each case, the following attributes were found common to at least two of the three sites. This Attributes section serves as a checklist of promising practices for use in designing, implementing, and sustaining interactive galleries.

Getting Started: Commencement

❑ Seek **high-level internal museum advocates** for an interactive education gallery, e.g., Board Members/Trustees, Director, community museum supporters.

❑ Seek **opportunities for an interactive gallery** concurrent with **museum new construction or renovation**.

Defining Family Learning: Research Base

❑ **Select a theoretical research base**: museum education, art education, creative play, concepts/skills-based learning, social interaction, styles of learning, family learning research.

❑ Determine the **intention you have for including family learning** in the institution.

Conceptualization and Learning: What's Your Big Idea?

❑ **Know your audience**: identify age ranges for the children in families and whether adults will be independent learners along with families in the interactive space.

❑ **Know your intentions for your audience**: identify how you imagine children and adults will interact together in the space—individually, as small groups, as larger groups.

❑ Host **charrette and or community/education focus groups**.

❑ **Travel to other family learning galleries:** art museums and other cultural institutions.

❑ **Maximize availability of expertise** at all levels: education experts, early childhood learning experts, experience of museum educators, focus groups, teachers, parents, and children.

❑ Use **child development research**.

❑ Seek **expertise in areas of education pedagogy**.

❑ Vary approaches for **different styles of learning**.

❑ Consider **intergenerational learning** as **another dimension of family learning**.

A Focus on Art: Object-based Approach

❑ Select an **intentional plan for referencing art**: reference to vs. inclusion of original works of art.

❑ Select objects or areas of the collections/exhibitions that make a **direct connection with the activities**.

❑ **Involve curatorial staff members** in selecting art references/objects.

Frist Art Museum   HIGH   HIGH MUSEUM OF ART ATLANTA   SPEED ART MUSEUM   INSTITUTE of Museum and Library SERVICES   audience focus   Institute for Learning Innovation

www.artmuseumfamilyspaces.org

Design and Build: From Outline through Fabrication

DESIGN
- ❏ Consider that **design reflects the times in which it is created**: high tech vs. manipulative.
- ❏**Establish a project manager**—if you manage the gallery project, plan for additional staff to assume other duties.
- ❏Select a **designer and fabricator that have a common desire to collaborate, listen, meet budgets and deadlines, and provide post-build customer service.**

- ❏ **Include meeting budget/timelines and post-build customer service (warranty/service) in the contract.**
- ❏Establish a **balance between the social interactions provided by activities** designed: independent, small group, high, moderate, calm.
- ❏ Provide **experiences** for a variety of **learning styles**.
- ❏Provide the **manipulative activities visitors seek the most** in balance with high-tech activities; use a higher technology level IF it is the best way to present a big idea.
- ❏**Avoid gratuitous interactivity**: e.g., pushing buttons for the sake of movement. Consider designs **with renewal in mind**, especially if you are planning for ongoing change vs. complete renovation.
- ❏ If accommodating school groups, **plan for optimum spacing for different sizes of groups**.
- ❏ Plan for **accessible storage/clean-up areas within the interactive space**.
- ❏ Plan for **ergonomics within the design** for adults as well as children.

BUILD
- ❏ Establish **lines of communication between project manager, designer, and fabricator**.
- ❏ Establish **shared, documented expectations between project manager, designer, and fabricator: for quality, aesthetic, and function**.
- ❏ Establish **consistent, frequent timelines for check-in** via electronic technology.
- ❏ **Test all materials** for durability over time and unexpected usages by participants.
- ❏ **Build to industrial standards** without looking industrial.

Funding and Budget

FUNDING
- ❏ **Seek Board of Trustees' support**—financially, conceptually, and for the integrity of the idea.
- ❏ **Plan time to seek initial funding** and time to seek secondary funding in the process.
- ❏ **Work with the Development Department.**

BUDGET

- ❏ Include a **sustainability/renewal budget** from the inception of the project.
- ❏ Create an annual line-item budget that **keeps the gallery sufficiently fresh, appealing, and up to date.**
- ❏ Ask for **a range of budget options** from designers/fabricators.
- ❏ Keep **funding between design and fabrication in balance.**
- ❏ Create a budget with a **range of flexibility** for **unexpected expenses and changes.**
- ❏ **Hold back spending too much too early.**
- ❏ **Establish a contingency fund.**
- ❏ Constantly **monitor invoicing and expenditures.**

Evaluation

- ❏ Include **beta testing/field testing/piloting** stations during original build and renovation.
- ❏ Include evaluation components **from the start** of the process.
- ❏ Select an **evaluation approach**: visitor studies, formative and summative evaluation components.
- ❏ **Train interactive gallery staff** in pragmatic but valid/reliable evaluation methods.
- ❏ Include **evaluation as a programming process.**

Sustainability

- ❏ Consider the interactive gallery as a **sustainable component of the museum mission.**
- ❏ **Host museum staff and Board of Trustees meetings** in the interactive space.
- ❏ Plan for **specific interactive gallery marketing strategies.**
- ❏ **Advertise in local parent/family magazines.**
- ❏ **Gauge the level of visitor needs**: approach visitors in balance with their perceived needs.

Renewal

- ❏ **Assess whether an activity/station is past its prime** or fresh to **first-time participants.**
- ❏ **Sustain a renewal budget.**
- ❏ **Place renewal efforts on your calendar** as if they were appointments.

Maintenance

- ❏ Provide a **safe interactive gallery** first and foremost—consider current climate/health concerns.
- ❏ Plan for a **significant amount of time for cleaning and disinfecting.**
- ❏ Budget for and **include technology support for any high-tech** components.
- ❏ When providing art materials, **provide safe but professional-grade art materials** that aren't readily available in the school or home environment.
- ❏ **Deliver on promises: quality, cleanliness, safety.**

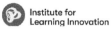

Sample Heat Map for
Balancing Family Gallery Activities

Sample Heat Map

	Entry	Found Object	Puppet/ Story	Imagin Spaces	Blocks/ Architec	Leaving a Mark
ENERGY LEVEL	Warm	Cool	Warm	Hot	Cool	Cool
SELF-EVIDENCE	High	Mod	Mod	High	High	High
SENSORY PAY-OFF	Mod	High	High	High	High	High
INTELLECTUAL PAY-OFF	Low	High	High	High	High	High
SOCIAL-PAYOFF Interaction	Mod	Mod	High	High	Mod	Mod
NUMBER OF USERS	High	High	High	High	High	High
UNIQUENESS	High	High	Mod	High	Mod	Mod
FLEXIBILITY of USE	Low	High	Mod	High	Mod	High
TECHNOLOGY LEVEL	Mod	Low	Low	Low	Low	Low
MAINTENANCE	Mod	Low	Mod	Mod	Mod	Low
SAFETY	High	High	High	High	High	Mod
PHYSICAL ACCESSIBILITY	High	High	High	High	High	High
FAMILY-FRIENDLINESS	Low	High	High	High	Low	High
CRITICAL THINKING SKILLS						
Investigation	✓✓	✓✓	✓	✓✓✓	✓	✓✓
Experimentation	✓	✓✓	✓✓✓	✓✓✓	✓✓✓	✓✓
Imagination	✓✓	✓✓✓	✓✓✓	✓✓✓	✓✓✓	✓✓✓
Compare/Contrast	✓	✓✓	✓✓	✓✓	✓	✓✓
Flexible Thinking	✓	✓✓	✓✓✓	✓✓✓	✓✓	✓✓✓
Reflection	✓	✓✓	✓✓✓	✓✓	✓	✓✓✓
Details	✓✓✓	✓✓✓	✓✓	✓✓	✓✓✓	✓✓✓
Sorting/Grouping	✓✓	✓✓✓	✓✓	✓✓	✓✓✓	✓✓
Draw on Past Exper.	✓✓✓	✓✓✓	✓✓✓	✓✓	✓✓	✓

Sample Experience Matrix

Experience Matrix

EXPERIENCE	VALUES						AGE APPROPRIATE						INCLUSIVE FOR ALL & MULTISENSORY									"CREATE" SKILLS					"EXPERIENCE" SKILLS				
	Welcoming, Safe & Fun	Child-Centered	Child-Directed	Open Ended	Intuitive	Repeatable	Baby (Birth–1 year)	Toddler (1–3 years)	Preschooler (3–5 years)	Gradeschooler (5–8+ years)	Caregiver	Caregiver Collaboration	Physically Accessible	Cognitively Accessible	Diverse Representations	Visual Expression	Tactile Expression	Audio Expression–Full	Body Expression	Intense Sensory Experience	Mild Sensory Experience	Creativity	Play	Collaboration	Outcome Focused	Process Focused	Imagination	Empathy	Looking Closely	Self-Reflection	Collaborative Engagement
Filtered Sunlight	•	•	•	•	•	•	•	•	•	•	•	•	•	•		•	•		•	•	•	•	•			•	•		•		
The Sketch Pad	•	•	•	•	•	•		•	•	•	•	•	•	•		•	•			•	•	•	•			•	•		•	•	•
Color Windows	•	•	•	•	•	•	•	•	•	•	•	•	•	•		•	•				•	•	•			•	•		•		
Peek-a-boo Box	•	•	•	•	•	•	•	•	•	•	•	•	•	•		•	•				•	•	•			•	•		•		
Stomp Splash	•	•	•	•	•	•		•	•	•	•	•	•	•		•	•		•	•	•	•	•			•	•	•	•	•	•
Community Tree	•	•	•	•	•	•	•	•	•	•	•	•	•	•	•	•	•	•			•	•	•		•	•	•	•	•	•	•
Daydream Builder	•	•	•	•	•	•		•	•	•	•	•	•	•	•	•	•	•			•	•	•	•	•	•	•		•	•	•
Colossal Blocks	•	•	•	•	•	•		•	•	•	•	•	•	•	•	•	•		•		•	•	•			•	•		•		
Curiosity Cabinets	•	•	•	•	•	•		•	•	•	•	•	•	•	•	•	•				•	•	•			•	•		•		
Soundscape	•	•	•	•	•	•	•	•	•	•	•	•	•	•		•	•	•		•	•	•	•		•	•	•		•	•	•
Self Portrait	•	•	•	•	•	•		•	•	•	•	•	•	•	•	•	•	•			•	•	•		•	•	•		•	•	•
Doodle Drawer	•	•	•	•	•	•		•	•	•	•	•	•	•	•	•	•	•			•	•	•		•	•	•		•	•	•
Whisper Tube	•	•	•	•	•	•	•	•	•	•	•	•	•	•		•	•	•			•	•	•			•	•	•	•	•	•
Immersive Entry	•	•	•	•	•	•	•	•	•	•	•	•	•	•		•	•		•	•	•	•	•			•	•		•	•	•
Wonder Cove	•	•	•	•	•	•	•	•	•	•	•	•	•	•		•	•		•	•	•	•	•			•	•		•	•	•
Noodle Tunnel	•	•	•	•	•	•	•	•	•	•	•	•	•	•		•	•		•	•	•	•	•			•	•		•	•	•
Color Cubby	•	•	•	•	•	•	•	•	•	•	•	•	•	•		•	•		•	•	•	•	•			•	•		•	•	•
Living Artworks	•	•	•	•	•	•		•	•	•	•	•	•	•	•	•	•				•	•	•			•	•		•	•	•
Texture Canyon	•	•	•	•	•	•	•	•	•	•	•	•	•	•		•	•			•	•	•	•			•	•		•	•	•
Color Cavern	•	•	•	•	•	•	•	•	•	•	•	•	•	•		•	•			•	•	•	•			•	•		•	•	•
Noodle Forest	•	•	•	•	•	•	•	•	•	•	•	•	•	•		•	•			•	•	•	•			•	•		•	•	•
The Overlook	•	•	•	•	•	•	•	•	•	•	•	•	•	•		•	•			•	•	•	•			•	•		•	•	•

Index

About the Authors

Julia Forbes is the Shannon Landing Amos Head of Museum Interpretation at the High Museum of Art in Atlanta, Georgia. She manages the development of all materials (docent-led tours, audio tours, interpretive gallery tools, labels, mobile technologies, etc.) used by visitors to learn about the museum's permanent collection and special exhibitions, including the Greene Family Learning Gallery. Forbes has held education positions at the Smithsonian's National Portrait Gallery, Washington National Cathedral, the Walters Art Museum, and the Smithsonian's National Museum of American History. She has developed exhibitions in a team setting and participated in the creation of interactive spaces for families in a wide range of museum settings. She served as the Eastern Region Director in the Education Division of the National Art Education Association, is the vice president of the Association for Art Museum Interpretation, and was honored as the Eastern Museum Educator of the Year for 1998. She has degrees in art history and cultural anthropology from the University of California, Santa Barbara and a master's degree from the George Washington University in art history/museum training.

Forbes has more than thirty years of experience in developing activities for families in a dedicated space. From the National Museum of American History's Hands on History Room to Washington National Cathedral's Cathedral Medieval Workshop and two iterations of the High Museum's Greene Family Learning Gallery, she has deep expertise in thinking about how intergenerational learning and play impact children and their caregivers in the museum setting. Forbes has presented on this topic at all the major museum conferences and was one of the leads on the Institute of Museum and Library Services (IMLS) funded study *Family Learning in Interactive Galleries* published online in 2011.

Marianna Adams, president of Audience Focus Inc., has designed, managed, and implemented a wide range of visitor research, interpretive planning, and professional development across the country, Canada,

Bermuda, Mexico, and the European Union. Before creating Audience Focus in 2007, she was a senior researcher at the Institute for Learning Innovation in Annapolis, Maryland, for twelve years, totaling more than twenty-five years' experience in visitor research. Her consulting work draws on extensive experience working in museums and schools. She headed education departments at the Ringling Museum of Art, Sarasota, Florida, and Museum of Art, Ft. Lauderdale, Florida, served as National Principal's Initiative co-coordinator for the summer 1995 Teacher Institute at the National Gallery of Art, Washington, DC, and taught public and private school K–12, high school literature and composition, middle and high school art, and middle school social studies. She has served as adjunct faculty for the George Washington University Museum Education and Museum Studies programs, for the University of North Texas Museum Studies program, and for the Oregon State University Informal Science Education program. She is currently adjunct professor for the Bank Street College of Education Museum Leadership graduate program, a position she has held since 2008. She was the Educator-in-Residence at the Isabella Stewart Gardner Museum in Boston during the summer of 2014. Adams received her BA in art and English literature from Mercer University, an MA in art education and arts administration from the University of South Florida, and her EdD in education policy from the George Washington University.

Jeanine Ancelet has directed and conducted a variety of research and evaluation projects for museums and free-choice learning organizations nationally and internationally since 2006. Her primary interest is to advocate for visitors and program participants and effectively communicate their needs, interests, and values to the organizations that serve them. Ancelet specializes in projects involving families and teens, as well as studies focused on the use and value of new media and technology in museums and other free choice learning organizations. She previously worked as a researcher at the Institute for Learning Innovation before joining Audience Focus Inc. Ancelet also teaches both in university classrooms and within museums, helping students and practitioners better understand the role evaluation can play in their day-to-day work. She currently serves as an adjunct faculty member at George Washington University, coteaching a course on museum evaluation in the Museum Education department. Her degrees are from the University College London, Institute for Archaeology (MA in museum studies) and Indiana University Bloomington (BA in anthropology, BA in English).

CPSIA information can be obtained
at www.ICGtesting.com
Printed in the USA
BVHW010113070222
627812BV00003B/4